ARAGON
Poet of the French Resistance

ARAGON

Poet of the French Resistance

Edited by

HANNAH JOSEPHSON

and

MALCOLM COWLEY

DUELL, SLOAN AND PEARCE · NEW YORK

PRINTED IN THE UNITED STATES OF AMERICA
AMERICAN BOOK—STRATFORD PRESS, INC., NEW YORK

CONTENTS

INTRODUCTION

ON MAY 25, 1941, Louis Aragon wrote me: "Have we the right to foresee what will happen in 1942 and 1943?" It was a letter in which he spoke of standing in line for an hour and three-quarters for a loaf of bread, of the poems he had written, of the novel on which he was engaged, of his wife's stories. And then he went on to tell of the strange fate of his literary generation: "First we worked over the problem of language so carefully that nothing seemed worthy of it; nothing seemed worth while saying. We said *nothing* magnificently and with the greatest freedom of expression. And now we have found what we had to say, more than we had ever dreamed. Can we ever say it well enough?"

Even before he wrote this letter Aragon had "said it well enough," in his poems of heartbreak, in his poems to Elsa his wife and his country. Within a few months he was to become one of the leaders of the resistance movement, he was to show his gifts as an organizer, a polemicist, an editor, a critic, and a master of every poetic form, as he took his place in the forefront of the drive to liberate France. He had something to say, and he said it magnificently.

This book is presented by several of Aragon's friends in homage to the poet and the fighter, whose achievements in a period of terror and catastrophe may well give heart to men and women of good will everywhere. The selections have been made with a view to giving an example of every type of writing he produced during those four years, especially those that marked a stage in the war of the resistance.

Acknowledgments are due to Mrs. Helen Burlin, Mr. Eugene Jay Sheffer and Mr. Matthew Josephson for their translations of certain selections from Aragon's prose. To Mr. Peter Rhodes, who has provided the article on Aragon's place in the resistance movement, special thanks must be given for having assembled and brought over the prose material, much of it rare and all of it difficult to obtain. There was a division of labor between the two editors: Malcolm Cowley edited the poetry section; I edited the prose. The poets who have translated Aragon's verse need no acknowledgment from me; they have paid their own tribute as poets to a great poet.

HANNAH JOSEPHSON

POETRY

POET OF THIS WAR

MORE than anyone else, Louis Aragon is the poet of this war, as it was lost and won in western Europe. He is by no means the only war poet; in his own country, which enjoyed a poetic revival during the years of defeat, there are also Paul Eluard, Pierre-Jean Jouve, Jean Cassou, Henri Michaux, Loys Masson, Pierre Emmanuel, and Patrice de la Tour du Pin, to mention a few of the names that recur more than others. In England and America, it would be hard to count the poets in the armed forces, but most of them have written about the struggle in relation to themselves; in war as in peace they have continued taking their spiritual pulses. Aragon forgot himself in the struggle; he spoke for his invaded country. He is the one poet who has left a complete record of the wartime emotions that were felt in common, from the first shock of mobilization to the joy of liberated Paris.

As a poet, it was his good fortune to be French, that is, native of a country occupied by the Nazis, but one where they hoped to rule by fraud as well as force. They did not try to destroy French culture; nor did they imprison or execute most of the writers, as happened in Czechoslovakia and Poland. The poets continued to publish their work, such of it as passed the Vichy censorship. They also continued to revolt against the Germans and against their own semblance of a government; and thus, as poets, they had an advantage over the British and Americans who have been fighting the war in uniforms. The man in uniform feels that a responsibility has been lifted from his shoulders. It isn't his war, no matter how much he believes in it and how often he risks his life for victory; as always in the past, it is the generals' war and the soldiers' fight. But in France, in the early days of the Resistance, each man was fighting under his own orders, until he freely submitted himself to orders from his comrades. I remember that Aragon told me long ago, in the midst of his reaction from the other war, "An outlaw is braver than a soldier, because he acts for himself." In France, all the members of the Resistance were outlaws. Everything conspired to keep them from fighting: the press, the radio, the police, and their own self-interest. Throughout the country, men examined their consciences; and either they stayed safely at home or else they went back to war, not as soldiers in the beginning, but simply as men.

Poets write best as lonely men, as rebels. When they are speaking for a government or a ruling party—even if they regard it with utter devotion—their verse becomes formal, discreet, and stiff in the joints, like an old diplomat; or it avoids those qualities by assuming a false innocence, like that of Miss Millay's ballad about Lidice. The French poets of the Resistance had the advantage of speaking as individuals—that is one side of the picture —but they also acknowledged a social duty that poetry can assume only in times of confusion: against the efforts of their own government, they had to keep the spirit of freedom alive in their nation. This was a task that could not be performed by novels or essays or plays in the theatre (although some of them carried their secret messages) or speeches over the radio or articles in the newspapers (until the underground press was established); all these means of expression were closely censored. The poets discovered, however, that their own medium had opportunities not granted to the others; that, with its power of allusion, it could rouse emotions and lead toward courses of action scarcely to be hinted at in prose;

that, poems being short, they could be copied and passed from hand to hand, even learned by heart, as Aragon's poems were learned and recited; that in short it could play the same role poetry had played in Homeric times and in the Middle Ages.

Poetry in England and the United States does not usually try to perform a social function, and fortunately does not have to perform it. The poet here, whether soldier or civilian, usually writes not only as an individual, but also as one opposed to the mass of his countrymen. When he says "I," he means specifically the "not-they," the not-as-other-men. Aragon as an individual spoke in his wartime poems for all patriotic Frenchmen: when he said "I," he also meant "we." And this was true even in the poems he wrote during the first months of idleness and skepticism at the front, when he declared again and again, "I am not one of theirs":

> *I am not theirs because my human flesh*
> *Is not a pastry to be cut with the knife*
> *Because a river seeks and finds the sea*
> *Because my living needs a sister life.*

He was not theirs, in short, because *they* (who might be either German or French) had become inhuman through believing themselves superhuman. He was a man, like the other soldiers; and he spoke for them directly in their bewilderment, as he would also speak directly for the French nation in defeat. "For the French," said André Gide, whom Aragon would later attack—unjustly, I think—for his hesitations during the first year after the German invasion, "there are always, in every field (and so much the better), two poles, two tendencies, two parties; in our own field there is, on the one side, reflective poetry (I am using the word in its two senses of 'contemplative' and 'reflected as in a mirror') and, on the other side, direct poetry. . . . For all the splendors of cerebral poetry in France, it is from the other tendency, from direct poetry, that I am now expecting our renaissance: from the mood that inspired Aragon to write the poems in *Heartbreak*—" and he went on to quote the end of Aragon's "Unoccupied Zone," which was already famous in 1941:

> *Hour after hour, without relief*
> *I sought an ill-remembered grief*
> *Until the September dawn*
>
> *When lying in your arms awake*
> *I heard one singing at daybreak*
> *Outside, an old French song*
> *Then knew my sorrow, branch and root*
> *Its music like a naked foot*
> *Troubled the pool where silence lay nightlong.*

There is a fundamental simplicity about poems like this, in spite of their technical experiments, their involved rhyme schemes, their bold and sometimes obscure images. The emotion itself is always straightforward. Aragon in his poems was giving back their old meaning to words like "love" and "courage" and "country." "Permit me to say in public," he wrote in one poem, "that the sun is the sun"—and it was as if he was also saying that death is death, that love is love, that France in defeat is still his country, and that liberty is not merely an orator's expression, but something worth risking one's life to restore. He wrote in "Christmas Roses," which is a tribute to the first men executed for their part in the Resistance:

> *Noel, Noel! That faint sunrise*
> *Gave back to you, men of little faith,*
> *The love for which one willingly dies*
> *And the future that relives his death.*

The war gave back to Aragon the world in which words have a real meaning, even the tritest of the words that describe human experiences. He was like a traveler returning after years to his own countryside, in which everything is familiar and yet has a different value, being seen with different eyes. That explains the effect, in his best poems, of a complex situation reduced, after years, to a statement as simple as that of the old Scotch ballads. He was the Border minstrel of this war.

Even Aragon's principal fault becomes a virtue in his wartime poetry. He writes easily, with apparently endless powers of invention, but sometimes also with deliberate negligence, with a willingness to follow the rhyme or the image wherever they lead him, with a tendency to repeat himself where he would refuse to copy others. He has a power of concentration that shames those of us who need quiet and leisure for their best work, or any work at all. Aragon works anywhere, at any hour and in any company. I have seen him writing in bed, propped on his left elbow; writing under the grape arbor while boys were noisily mowing the lawn; writing in a corner of a room that was full of people talking English and sometimes interrupting him with a question; he would answer it, in English, and go on writing French prose. That was in the early summer of 1939, when he was three-fourths of the way through a novel, *The Century Was Young*. The novel was still unfinished when, after his return to Paris, the newspaper he edited was suppressed on August 25. Aragon had a week of leisure before entering the army, on September 2. During that week, with the world going to pieces, he wrote the last hundred pages of his book. He had the proofs with him at Dunkerque, and made corrections in them while waiting to be evacuated.

For the poetry he wrote during the war, his special gift was necessary. There was no time for self-questioning, for writhing in the pains of composition; there was not much time to write at all, except for a man like Aragon who could do his work in barracks, in trains, in waiting rooms, or on the beach at Dunkerque. Unlike less naturally gifted poets, he was able to set down his impressions and emotions as they came, so that his six volumes of wartime poetry became a month-by-month record of the struggle: the boredom and loneliness of the "phony war"; the grotesque horror of the German invasion, like Breughel's conception of hell; the utter weight of defeat, under which Aragon was among the first to stand erect; then the impulse for reëxamining French history, to find the real strength of the nation; and the growing power of the Resistance, which at first he merely suggested in his poems, but later mirrored frankly, so that his work was forbidden by the Vichy censors and he turned to writing ballads of combat to be printed in the underground newspapers or smuggled across the border and published in Switzerland; and at last the frantic joy of "Paris, Paris, of herself liberated" —all of it is there, in Aragon's verse.

II

It was the war that made Aragon a poet again. He had written a quantity of verse in his younger days; and after his trip to Russia, about 1930, he had written one long poem, "Red Front," that led to his being given a sentence of five years in prison for insulting the French flag; but the sentence had been suspended and Aragon had plunged into politics, journalism, and social fiction. In 1939 he was the editor of *Ce Soir*, a left-wing afternoon newspaper with a circulation of almost half a million, and, besides his early books, he was the author of two long social novels with a rather wide sale and a generally favorable reception from the critics; a third novel, as I said, was almost finished. Then, at the end of August, the newspaper was suppressed; the new novel was not exactly suppressed—it was too soon for that—but difficulties were put in the way of its publication; and the author, at the age of forty-two, was drafted into the army, where Military Intelligence was instructed to keep a careful watch on him. His double career in literature and journalism had come to a full stop.

He served through the "phony war" and the invasion of France as an "auxiliary doctor" (he had been graduated from medical school but had never taken his interneship), and he ranked from beginning to end as an *adjutant,* roughly equivalent to an American warrant officer. At first he was punished for his political opinions by being assigned to a labor regiment composed chiefly of Czech and Spanish refugees, people not trusted to bear arms at the front but merely to dig fortifications. Later he managed to get himself transferred to a light motorized division, but, until the fighting began, he had very little to do. In his loneliness he began writing poetry again. It was poetry composed with an astonishing technical virtuosity; and also, what is more important, it expressed the bewilderment and the longing for home of the whole French army.

Aragon was finishing a poem ("The Interrupted Poem") on the early morning of May 10, 1940, when he received orders to join an armored detachment that was crossing the frontier into Belgium in advance of the main Allied forces. More than once during the campaign that followed, the detachment had to fight its way from behind the German lines. At last the whole division was surrounded, with the army to which it belonged; and it was only "by a pretty improbable piece of luck," as Aragon wrote in a letter to his friends the Josephsons, that it managed to join the English forces on the beach at Dunkerque. Its equipment had to be abandoned there. All that Aragon carried with him to England, he wrote in another letter, was his sleeping bag, a few dry biscuits, his raincoat, and the half-corrected proofs of his novel.[1]

His division returned to France after spending one

[1] Meanwhile the printer's type of the novel had been destroyed, apparently in a bombing raid. The book was later reset from the proofs that Aragon had carried with him through the Battle of France. Enough passages were deleted to meet the censor's objections, and the novel was published at last, in 1942. It was almost immediately suppressed by the Germans—but all that is another story.—M. C.

night at Plymouth. It landed at Brest, received new equipment, and went back into the battle line at Vernon, on the lower Seine. From there it fought in the rearguard of the retreating French armies until it had reached the country south of the Loire. Aragon was taken prisoner at Angoulême, on the last day of the fighting, but he escaped under fire with six automobiles and thirty men. He was demobilized at the end of July and, his wife having joined him, they spent three weeks together in a pink château in the Limousin. By that time he had received the Croix de Guerre, with a divisional citation, for his exploits in Belgium; a second Croix de Guerre, with an army citation, for the fighting on the Loire; and the Médaille Militaire, one of the two highest French decorations, for his escape from the Germans. Later this collection of medals would save him more than once from arrest by the Vichy police.

His adventures after the French armistice and his achievements as an organizer for the underground movement are described at length in the chapter by Peter Rhodes. As for his poetic activity, which is properly my subject, it falls into three separate periods. First came the weeks that Louis and Elsa Aragon spent in the pink château and their four months in Carcassonne—the months, precisely, when French poets and their countrymen were stunned by the sudden collapse, as it then appeared, of a whole civilization; when they had no idea of what they could usefully do, either as writers or as patriots. During this period, Aragon wrote a long letter to the Josephsons, at the end of which he said:

In the Occupied Zone my books, like those of many other French writers, can no longer be sold, while in the Free Zone that question does not even arise, since all the printed copies are in Paris and the publisher is forbidden to ship them across the line of demarcation. Looking forward, I can see no possibility of earning my living as a writer; and it is even a question whether I can find any other sort of work. By being very careful with what remains of my army pay, I think we can live here in a small way until November 1. After that, who knows? . . .

I am writing poems, and as long as the fighting lasted I was still able to publish them from time to time. I still write them, but I keep them for myself. Elsa, whose books are unobtainable like mine, has just begun a long story, and I want her to finish it, because the beginning is wonderfully vivid. But it takes a great deal of courage to write without knowing what will happen to one's work. What a terrible road since the days we spent together! Note that the rest of this letter would be false to my meaning if you concluded from it that I have become pessimistic. I believe on the contrary that God moves in a mysterious way and that the gate is strait through which we must pass. In my country, even when it is unfortunate, even when it is crushed, I have a confidence that there is no way of expressing except by deeds; and there is nothing to change in what I told you there in your country house, of which I dream today as if it were some image of childhood or a scene from a novel. . . .

Your old friend (my hair is now completely white) who hasn't forgotten you.

Louis

The poems he was writing at the time were battle pieces like the "Tapestry of the Great Fear" and the "Song for a Barrel Organ"; or they were songs of France in defeat like "Richard II Forty" and "Richard Coeur-de-Lion" and "The Lilacs and the Roses"—all with the weight of emotion and the simplicity of old ballads, but with images drawn from our own age of total warfare. If he spoke of French roses, they were:

Flowers that gave the lie to soldiers passing
On wings of fear, a fear importunate as a breeze,
And gave the lie to the lunatic push-bikes and the ironic
Guns and the sorry rig of the refugees.

All these poems were written for himself, but Aragon showed them to other writers who had gathered in Carcassonne; copies passed from hand to hand. Somebody sent an imperfect copy of one poem to the literary supple-

~ 11 ~

ment of *Le Figaro,* which was then being published in Lyons, in the Unoccupied Zone. "The Lilacs and the Roses" appeared in the issue of September 21, 1940 (and appeared again, with the author's corrections, in the issue of September 28). Many people expected that the newspaper would be fined or even suppressed for its temerity in printing a poem that said in simple words what everybody was feeling. The censor, however, had no objections to offer. Poems like those that Aragon was writing found protection in the ambiguous position of the Vichy government: they were patriotic and Vichy, too, claimed to be patriotic; they appealed to French traditions and Vichy was also appealing to them; they were the work, in Aragon's case, of a veteran three times decorated and Vichy was trying to conciliate the other veterans. The result was that more and more of Aragon's new poems appeared, in *Poésie 41* and other legally printed magazines; and many other French poets began to write in a similar vein.

That was the first winter of what Pierre Seghers, the editor of *Poésie,* would afterwards describe as the conspiracy of poets, *la conspiration des poètes.* Others, including Gide, spoke of a poetic renaissance, and they had good reasons for using the phrase, for poetry was receiving more attention than at any other period since the flowering of the Romantic movement. But the renaissance this time had a political or, to be more exact, a national basis. When writers discovered how much they could say in verse without having their work suppressed, and how carefully poems were being read, they turned away from prose; novelists became poets; former poets began writing verse again; new poets were discovered by the score. As Aragon said in the long letter that he wrote me, in English, after the liberation of France: "The new poetry was in fact a conspiracy among certain writers and poets, conscious and unconscious, to put into our literature the necessary patriotic flavor and express just what our masters wanted not to be told."

His poems of this second period were written slowly (he had more leisure during those months than afterwards or before), with great formal inventiveness and technical finish, and with a wealth of historical allusions. He couldn't attack the Germans directly, but he could refer to the sorrows of France during the Hundred Years War, and his readers understood. He rebellion was more clearly expressed with every month that passed. After the Germans began shooting hostages, he could no longer express himself within the strict limits of "legal" literature. As the result of one angry poem, "X . . . Français," written to commemorate an engineer named Jacques Bonsergent, who had been executed for helping to organize the Resistance, all the French reviews were "advised" by Vichy not to print any more of Aragon's work. He continued writing for them, under a dozen different pseudonyms—and occasionally under his own name as well—but most of his poems were now printed either in Switzerland, after being smuggled across the border, or else in the newspapers of the underground. And the poet himself had to go underground, after the invasion of North Africa. He said in a letter from which I have quoted already: "When, on November 11, 1942, the Italians crossed the border and entered Nice, we left without regard to other considerations and went under the deep and pleasant cover of illegality."

In that same letter, after describing his work for the Resistance—but Peter Rhodes tells that part of the story —he tried to give me a picture of France before the liberation. He said in English that keeps a French flavor:

We had received orders *not* to do any local job, *not* to come in touch with local party members, and so on. But we couldn't, after a certain moment, keep from helping the people around us: because that last year you can't imagine what France was like. My God, it was a repayment for everything in life! And people can slander and chitchat and loathe us, but we have seen that, the heroic moment when everybody was ready at every moment to die for anybody, people they didn't even know, provided that they were against the common enemy. You must believe me . . . that it is by no means a manner of speech if I say that in those incredibly long and bloody months life became a song for all of us: and you know, in the best of songs there are certainly tears, but how beautiful the voice and the eyes of people appear when singing, they can't stop themselves crying!

In those days when life itself was a song, Aragon was still writing poems. He even wrote a very long poem, *Le Musée Grévin,* in which Laval, Hitler, Mussolini, and Pétain were presented as figures in a waxworks museum. First printed by Midnight Editions, the book-publishing house of the Resistance, *Le Musée Grévin* was reprinted a hundred times all over France, usually as a folded leaflet in very small type. Aragon also wrote, during this period, a number of songs and ballads for the French Partisans. These appeared in dozens of underground papers; then, after the liberation, they were collected and published in Paris as *Reveille in France (La Diane Française).*

Writing for his comrades in their own clandestine press, Aragon was at last free to say exactly what he felt about the foreign invaders and the traitors at home. But along with this privilege he had a duty: he had to make every line of verse contribute directly to the struggle. Space in the underground papers was precious, and any poem that appeared in them, or any poem printed as a leaflet and distributed at the risk of death, had to be written and judged by other standards than those of literature in the abstract. All the songs and ballads in *La Diane Française* show the exultant grief of those days when "everybody was ready at every moment to die for anybody." Many of them, but especially the "Ballad of One Who Sang at the Stake," enjoyed a popularity that poets might dream about here, but never achieve in these days when poetry is practiced as a private art. In the time of the maquis, they were learned by heart and recited at campfires; after the liberation, they were read from the stage of the Comédie Française; they were heard over the radio and even on phonograph records. . . . This sort of popularity makes us distrust them a little, as poems. There is no doubt that some of them will live for a long time: the "Prelude" and "Elsa at the Mirror" and "Christmas Roses" among others; but I should judge that the future will prefer the "legal" poems that Aragon wrote in the first days of defeat. In them the need for speaking his mind without violating the rules of the Vichy censor was like a new difficulty, a new convention superimposed on the old poetic conventions. The devices he found for meeting it gave his poems of that period more depth, more richness, more density than he could achieve in ballads where his whole meaning had to be clear at a first glance.

In all, Aragon managed to write and publish six books of poetry during the war, not counting the *Cantique à Elsa,* which was published in Algiers and later included in a longer volume. Of the others, only the first, *Heartbreak (Le Crève-Coeur),* was printed legally in France during the occupation; it was promptly suppressed by the Germans. *Les Yeux d'Elsa, Brocéliande,* and *En Français dans le Texte* all appeared in Switzerland; a few copies of each were smuggled across the border with the complicity of the French censor at Annemasse. The fifth volume was *Le Musée Grévin,* printed illegally by the Resistance; the sixth and last, which appeared in Paris after the liberation, was *La Diane Française.* Together the six books are a record of the wartime emotions of French soldiers and civilians—and of all those in Allied countries who were committed to the war—such as no other poet has even attempted to give. All of Aragon's virtues and even his faults conspired together to make the story complete. I know of nothing in English or American literature to compare with it, except the record of the Civil War that Walt Whitman left in his *Drum-Taps.*

III

It is a spontaneous tribute to Aragon that so many poets, English and American, have undertaken to translate his work. They all knew in the beginning, and they learned again before completing their task, that poetry is in the strict sense untranslatable. Even prose is difficult or impossible to translate when it is something more than a statement of facts or ideas and also tries to suggest emotions. The most a translator can do is to construct what is as nearly as possible an English equivalent of the original French. In rare cases the equivalent may be better than the original. I shouldn't make that claim for any of the translations in this volume, but a few of them are remarkable achievements. I might call special attention to John Hayward's "More Beautiful Than Tears," a poem which I had at first judged to be too purely French for even a rough English approximation, let alone an accurate version like Hayward's; and to Louis Mac-Neice's "Richard Coeur-de-Lion," which is not only a fine English poem in itself, but also a careful rendering of the French, in the rhymes as well as in the meaning.

Rhyme was one of the principal difficulties that all the translators had to face. There have always been more French than English rhymes; the fact is that the number of good rhymes in spoken English has been decreasing from generation to generation, as English grammar became more and more simplified. Poets who don't want to seem archaic can no longer couple *task* with *did ask* or *death* with *burieth*. For American poets the problem is still more difficult, since our increasingly urban speech has dropped so many of the Saxon monosyllables referring to country life. *Fen, bog, copse, swale, snath, helve:* all these are good rhyming words in England, but what American could use them naturally in poems dealing with mechanized warfare?

Among French poets, Aragon is distinguished for his use of rhyme, which he employs according to a system of his own. As in classical French prosody, he alternates masculine with feminine rhymes, but he uses his own (or rather Guillaume Apollinaire's) definition of masculine and feminine: his masculine rhymes are those ending in a vowel or a nasalized consonant; his feminine rhymes end in a sounded consonant, whether or not it is followed by a mute *e*. Thus, in one of his poems *ciel* rhymes with *elle* and *querelles,* in defiance of all rhyming dictionaries (but not in defiance of spoken French); it serves as his feminine rhyme. *Pas* rhymes with *verra* and *derobât* and serves as his masculine rhyme. The whole poem, "La Rose et le Réséda," consists of sixty-four lines, each having one of those two endings: a pattern almost impossible to duplicate in English without a complete sacrifice of meaning. It seemed better to most of the translators in this volume to sacrifice some of the rhymes, or to use false rhymes and alliteration, while retaining as much as possible of the sense.

Meter was another problem that the different translators solved in different fashions. Aragon's favorite meter, like that of most French poets, is the twelve-syllable line with a pause after the sixth syllable: the alexandrine. It is a little lighter in effect than English hexameter, and a little longer than the common English measure consisting of ten syllables, five of them accented: the "heroic line." The commonest solution was to write heroic lines with one or two extra syllables. But Stephen Spender, in his version of "Paris," counted syllables as in French, instead of accents as in English verse; and the translation of "Christmas Roses" follows much the same method.

A lesser difficulty that the translators solved in their different fashions was that of punctuation. Aragon doesn't punctuate at all; he merely capitalizes the first letter in each line, and the first letter of each sentence if it starts inside the line. Spender, in his version of "Paris," followed the author's system strictly, whereas other translators inserted all the punctuation marks, as in English verse; and still others, including myself, adopted the somewhat cowardly compromise of inserting punctuation marks in the middle of lines, to make the meaning clear, but omitting the commas and periods and semicolons at the end of the lines, where the typography itself serves as a sort of punctuation.

But the real point I wanted to make in this necessarily technical discussion was that, in spite of their different personalities and different methods, all the translators were trying hard to render Aragon exactly; and that his own personality, his own style, his own story are strong enough to persist essentially unchanged in all the translations. We owe a considerable debt to the men and women who made them,[2] for without their work the present collection would have been impossible.

MALCOLM COWLEY

[2] And a special debt to Rolfe Humphries, who made preliminary English drafts of almost all the poems in *Le Crève-Coeur* and *Les Yeux d'Elsa* and final drafts of many. We likewise owe a debt of gratitude to the magazines that printed Aragon's poems in translation. Twelve of the poems in this volume appeared as a group in the autumn, 1945, issue of the *Sewanee Review*. Five of them were printed at various times in the *New Republic*, and four of them in *Poetry*, including the translations by George Dillon and William Jay Smith. *Tricolor* printed the two longest poems: "More Beautiful Than Tears," in John Hayward's translation, and "I Salute You, My France," by Grace Wallace. "Christmas Roses" appeared in *Mademoiselle* and an earlier version of "Night at Dunkerque" in *Harper's Magazine*. Parts of my introduction to the poems were published by the *New Republic* and by the *Saturday Review*. We extend our thanks to the editors of all these magazines for their cooperation.—M. C.

TWENTY YEARS AFTER

Time has refound its lumbering old wain
And yoked its slow red oxen. Autumn again
The sun digs holes among the golden leaves
X-rayed October shivered once but sleeps

Carolingian days. We are do-nothing kings
Our dreams keep time to the cattle sauntering
We hardly know men die at the edge of town
Our sunrise deeds forgotten at sundown

We wander through evacuated homes
No chains to clank, no winding sheets, no groans
We are noontide spectres, ghosts in broad daylight
And phantoms from a life where love was known

We fetch our habits after twenty years
From oblivion's cloakroom. A thousand prisoners
Make the old gestures, stiff and obsolete
In cells where they feel neither cold nor heat

Men talk in mechanical phrases, lay aside
This time again their ballads and their pride
What clings to their lips is an imbecile hi-de-ho
Heard once too often over the radio

Time hardly enough for a boyhood. Twenty years
And now in middle life we must pay arrears
Watching the conscripts who were babies then
All innocent march out with us again

Twenty years after, words of Dumas *père*
Ironically we hear this title where
Our lifetime is inscribed, and then we swerve
In dreams to meet the shadow of her we love

There is only one, tender and loveliest
Only one passion, one hope and one distress
Still shining from the brown October haze
I wait for her to write, I count the days

You have had of my life only the riper part
O my wife, only the pensive years that were
Stingily dealt us, but the friends we knew
In speaking of us always said, Those two

No, you lost nothing of that bad young man
Now vanished like a letter in the sand
Like a sign peeling from a rain-washed wall
You never knew that shade, that nothing at all

A man changes as clouds change in the sky
You tenderly passed your hand over my eyes
And on my forehead smoothed the lines away
Your fingers pausing where the hair was gray

My love, my love, there is nothing left but you
Now at this hour of my sad twilight
When I lose at once the thread of what I write
And of life itself and the will to speak or do
Because I wanted to say, I love you always
And the words hurt when spoken without you.

Malcolm Cowley

I WAIT FOR HER LETTER AT SUNSET

Under a cretonne sky
Pompadour style and how
A little truck comes sailing
Echo deceives us. What
Is this song swallowed up
By dusk in the haunted wood
Where a whole regiment dreams
Bivouacked in shadow
Deep, deep in autumn weather?

And how the wartime hours
We kill at Crouy-sur-Ourcq
Die painfully. And you are
My vulture and my dove
Oh, mail-truck of the mist
Oh, melancholy cupid
Dawdling up the drive
Oh, barkentine, forsake
The plowed earth, sail the skies
Have you seen my mistress there
Sad, sad and dreaming?

And this autumnal gilt
These ormulu riches are
My love's terrestrial dress?
What does she tell me, wind
What does she tell me? Stay
Stay as you did before
The battles in the east.

No mail, the sergeant says.

Rolfe Humphries and Malcolm Cowley

~ 21 ~

THE TIME OF CROSSWORD PUZZLES

O sun of sleepless midnight, solitude
Of husbandless houses where they lie awake
Spouses of terror, counting round their beds
The monsters that stand leering till daybreak

Who was it that unchained the banished fear
Put sand on the roof, insomnia in their hearts
And daubed the windowpanes with panic blue?
Nobody any more consults the cards

Keep dancing, wizards, on your briary heath
They will not seek your love-philtres again
Love bowed their heads more humbly than a prayer
When the East Station swallowed up their men

Women who know at last as we ourselves
The paradise lost of our unknotted limbs
Do you hear the voice that murmurs, Only you
As lips bestow a kiss on the hollow winds?

Absence abominable, absinthe of the war
Once more we drink that bitter counterfeit
And yet our limbs were fused not long ago
I sensed for you whatever your body did

Too little have we prized those double hours
Too little asked if our dreams were counterparts
Too lightly probed the look in troubled eyes
Too seldom talked of our concurrent hearts

But only as a secret to share with you
Do I see the world in its other countenance
When rain-clouds grizzle the aging face of day
And now the midnight trees begin to dance

Listen. In the night my heartbeats call
I grope in bed for your presence unawares
And everything slips away. Except for you
Nothing else matters. I am not one of theirs

I am not theirs because I would have to be
Like Ligier's carved half-skeleton at Bar
Fleshless down to the waist, but holding up
To the high window his poor barbarous heart

I am not theirs because my human flesh
Is not a pastry to be cut with the knife
Because a river seeks and finds the sea
Because my living needs a sister life

I am not one of theirs because the shade
Exists for lovers, sunlight for the trees
Winds for the poplars scattering their seed
On the bee-encumbered, honey-laden breeze

I am yours. I am yours only. I adore
Your footprint and the hollow where you lay
Your slipper dropped, your handkerchief. Go sleep
My frightened child. I promise to lie awake

Here until dawn. The medieval night
Has draped this broken universe with black
If not for us, the storm will some day pass
The time of crossword puzzles will come back

Malcolm Cowley

LITTLE SUITE FOR LOUDSPEAKER

I

Hilversum, Kalundborg, Brno, the loud world over
Monday to Sunday, the idiot radio
Spits germs on Mozart, dedicates to you
Silence, its endlessly insulting brew

Loud Jove in love with Io, queen of cows
Has left her tethered by the waterside
She hears by radio at eventide
Cracklings of static from the hidden spouse

Like her—for this is war—hearing the Voice
Men stay in their stupidity and caress
Toulouse, PTT, Daventry, Bucharest

Their hope, the good old hope of former days
Interrogates the ether, which replies
That Carter's little liver pills are best.

Rolfe Humphries

II

Ah, speak to me of love, waves, little waves
For even the heart in shadow has its cries
Ah, speak to me of love. We spend the days
Doubting, foreboding, writing to ourselves
Ah, speak of love while letters make their slow
Round trip from Paris to this wilderness

You will speak of love. The ballad and the waltz
Will mock at space and absence. A ball that she
And I have never seen is opening now
The violins would make a poet swoon
You will speak of love with elemental words
While night and sky unfold to a juke-box tune

Speak to me not of love, for now my heart
Drowns out the melodies that set it beating
Speak not of love. What is she doing there
Too near, too far away, O martyred days
Speak not of love. A fire hums on the hearth
And the smell of kisses rises from the blaze

Yes, speak of love again and let it rhyme
With dove or soul or anything you say
Now speak of love for all the rest is crime
And men gone crazy frighten off the birds
From the bare boughs that winter rains begrime
Where the nests resemble pleasures flown away

Speak once of love and you have spoken of her
She is all music and the secret garden
Where Renaud lost his heart to the enchantress
Yet never spoke of love, oh, silly paladin
So like ourselves before we went to war
Against the paynim and their sultan Saladin

We shall speak of love as long as suns go down
As long as spring comes back with chattering swallows
I shall speak of love in bed with dreams for pillows
Where you and I shall be a golden crown

And you will tell me, Put the paper down.

Rolfe Humphries and Malcolm Cowley

~ 25 ~

THE WALTZ OF THE TWENTY-YEAR-OLDS

Good for the wind, good for the night, good for the cold
Good for the march and the bullets and the mud
Good for legends, good for the stations of the cross
Good for absence and long evenings. Funny ball
At which I danced and, children, you will dance
To the same dehumanized orchestral score
Good for fear, good for machine guns, good for rats
Good as good bread and good as simple salad

But here is the rising of the conscript sun
The waltz of the twenty-year-olds sweeps over Paris

Good for a shot of brandy at dawn and the anguish
    before the attack
Good for the waiting, the storm and the patrols
Good for night silence under rocket flares
Good for youth passing and the rusting heart
Good for love and death, good to be forgotten
In the rain and shadow cloaking the battlefields
Child soldiers trundled in no other bed
But the ditch already tailored to their measure

The twenty-year-old waltz sweeps through the bistros
And breaks like a laugh at the entrance to the Métro

Army classes of yesterday, vanished dreams
Fourteen, Fifteen, Sixteen: listen. They hum
Like us the trite refrain, like us believe it
And like us in those days, may God forgive them
They value more than their lives a single moment
Of drunkenness, of folly, of delight
What do they know of the world? Does living mean
Quite simply, Mother, to die very young?

Good for this, good for that. My good friends I am leaving
Twenty years old. Good for the armed forces.

Ah, the waltz begins and the dancer buys the same
Eternal trinkets from the Arab peddlers
But this time sings the daughter of Madelon
I have used up forty years. Their twenty are coming
   close
Boulevard Saint-Germain and Rue Saint-Honoré
With flags in their lapels the class of Forty
Hears the word Good repeated in golden English
I want to believe with them that life is swell

I will forget, I will forget, forget, forget
The waltz of the twenty-year-olds will sweep away
      My forty years in the year 1940.

Rolfe Humphries and Malcolm Cowley

SANTA ESPINA

I remember a tune we used to hear in Spain
And it made the heart beat faster, and we knew
Each time as our blood was kindled once again
Why the blue sky above us was so blue

I remember a tune like the voice of the open sea
Like the cry of migrant birds, a tune which stores
In the silence, after the notes, a stifled sob
Revenge of the salt seas on their conquerors

I remember a tune which was whistled at night
In a sunless time, an age with no wandering knight
When children wept for the bombs and in catacombs
A noble people dreamt of the tyrants' doom

It bore in its name the sacred thorns which pierced
The brow of a god as he hung upon the gallows
The song that was heard in the ear and felt in the flesh
Reopened the wound in his side and revived his sorrows

No one dared to sing to the air they hummed
All the words were forbidden and yet I know
Universe ravaged with inveterate pox
It was your hope and your month of Sundays. O

Vainly I seek its poignant melody
But the earth has now but operatic tears
The memory of its murmuring waters lost
The call of stream to stream, in these deaf years

O Holy Thorn, Holy Thorn, begin again
We used to stand as we heard you long ago
But now there is no one left to renew the strain
The woods are silent, the singers dead in Spain

I would like to believe that there is music still
In that country's heart, though hidden underground
The dumb will speak and the paralytics will
March one fine day to the cobla's triumphant sound

The crown of blood, the symbol of anguish and sorrow
Will fall from the brow of the Son of Man that hour
And man will sing loudly in that sweet tomorrow
For the beauty of life and the hawthorn tree in flower.

Kenneth Muir

SPRING

The long cries from the barges on the Scheldt
Wakened the night, like a warm girl, from slumber:
The radio sang a common little number
So love-pervaded that it touched the heart.

Beside a dreaming girl a man was lying
Sprawled on the deck; and was I dreaming too?
Somebody's voice called out, "Be seeing you."
Somebody muttered, "In Norway men are dying."

Men of the border, whose longing goes along
Like slow canals, to lands of foreign name:
Here Belgium ends, here France begins; and here
The flags are different, but the sky the same.

This was the year we waited very long
For the month whose eyes are violets, lovely May,
When the wine runs fresher in exhausted veins,
When apple blossoms make a veil for the day.

We have waited him so long, the god reborn,
The god who dies of love before the fall,
So long, so long imprisoned, we have lost
Desire or power to believe at all.

Earth-colored, deaf to the world, in mask and helmet,
With leather over our soldier hearts, we spent
The winter under arms, guarding chimeras,
Our packs were heavy and our backs were bent.

What a laugh, to think of people sleeping naked
Of kids on scooters in another world.
Euler, for all his blindness, could discover
New laws of motion as the planets whirled,

But we were eyeless, loveless, brainless phantoms,
Ghosts parted from ourselves, waiting in vain
Renewal; our discoveries were only
Old oaths and blasphemies, mouthed over again.

Shall we not come to life, O false dead men?
Is there no opening door, no great wind blowing,
No coming spring, no perfume in the air,
Like a caress, no sound of overthrowing?

And yet for whom, beloved, should the flowers
Blossom, except for you? The April spell
Means nothing to me, with you gone, and May,
However lovely, is an utter hell.

Bring back my heaven, my music, O my wife,
Without whom all is colorless and vain,
The spring a sandy waste, a desert life,
The sunshine insult, and the shadow pain.

Rolfe Humphries

THE INTERRUPTED POEM

Without its mate the bird
In the midst of carnage sings
As we in battle too
But where, bright love, are you?
Laden with lambs and jars
Here come the stubborn sweet
Lettuce-green fields of May
Like statues in a church
Of holy men and beasts
Painted with every grace

Season of colors, future
Still shapeless at the dawn
Wounded and weak and wan
What dream in the heavens outrides
The night that will not be gone?
You tremble as before
And now our divided hearts
Take up the laggard beat
One spring is like another
Our spring is being together

The sun is perplexed and pale
Sad as a house for sale
A fire that will not rekindle
Or lips that cannot be kissed
Curtains are drawn this morning
Once more falls the Flanders mist
Our spring is long delayed
But the skies are not hard to read
When we are not together
Why should the air be tender?

And what is happy love?
For being in its thrall
Verona's lovers paid
Drinking black veronal
Yours is this cup of blue
This sudden trill, my song
Among the armored cars
It rises clear and pure
To pass above the walls
Above the friends we knew
My only love, my wound

. . . . . .
. . . . . .

May 10, 1940, at sunrise

Rolfe Humphries and Malcolm Cowley

THE LILACS AND THE ROSES

O months of blossoming, months of transfigurations,
May without cloud and June stabbed to the heart,
I shall not ever forget the lilacs or the roses
Nor those the spring has kept folded away apart.

I shall not ever forget the tragic sleight-of-hand,
The cavalcade, the cries, the crowd, the sun,
The lorries loaded with love, the Belgian gifts,
The road humming with bees, the atmosphere that spun,
The feckless triumphing before the battle,
The scarlet blood the scarlet kiss bespoke
And those about to die bolt upright in the turrets
Smothered in lilac by a drunken folk.

I shall not ever forget the flower gardens of France—
Illuminated scrolls from eras more than spent—
Nor forget the trouble of dusk, the sphinxlike silence,
The roses all along the way we went;
Flowers that gave the lie to soldiers passing
On wings of fear, a fear importunate as a breeze,
And gave the lie to the lunatic push-bikes and the ironic
Guns and the sorry rig of the refugees.

But what I do not know is why this whirl
Of memories always comes to the same point and drops
At Sainte-Marthe . . . a general . . . a black pattern,
A Norman villa where the forest stops;
All is quiet here, the enemy rests in the night
And Paris has surrendered, so we have just heard—
I shall never forget the lilacs nor the roses
Nor those two loves whose loss we have incurred:

Bouquets of the first day, lilacs, Flanders lilacs,
Soft cheeks of shadow rouged by death—and you,
Bouquets of the retreat, delicate roses, tinted
Like far-off conflagrations: roses of Anjou.

Louis MacNeice

TAPESTRY OF THE GREAT FEAR

This landscape, masterpiece of modern terror
Has sharks and sirens, flying fish and swordfish
And hydra-headed birds like Lerna's hydra
What are they writing, white on blue, in the sky?
Skimmers of earth, steel birds that stitch the air
To the stone houses, strident comet-birds
Enormous wasps like acrobatic matchsticks
That deck the flaming walls with primroses
Or flights of pink flamingos in the sun
Kermess in Flanders, witches at their Sabbath
On a broomstick the Messerschmitt rides down
Darkness at noon, night of the new Walpurgis
Apocalyptic time. Space where fear passes
With all its baggage train of tears and trembling
Do you recognize the fields, the birds of prey?
The steeple where the bells will never ring
The farm carts draped with bedclothes. A tame bear
A shawl. A dead man dropped like an old shoe
Hands clutching the torn belly. A grandfather's clock
Roaming herds of cattle, carcasses, cries
Art bronzes by the roadside. Where will you sleep?
Children perched on the shoulders of strange men
Tramping off somewhere, while the gold of the barns
Gleams in their hair. Ditches where terror sits
The dying man in a cart who keeps asking
For herb tea, and complains of a cold sweat
A hunchbacked woman with a wedding dress
A birdcage that passed safely through the flames
A sewing machine. An old man. I can't walk
Just a step more. No, let me die here, Marie
Evening soars down with silent wingbeats, joining
A velvet Breughel to this Breughel of hell.[1]

Malcolm Cowley

[1] Pieter Breughel the Younger liked to paint the flames of the pit;
he was known as "Hell Breughel." His brother Jan the Elder, known
as "Velvet Breughel," liked to paint all that was most adorable on
earth and in heaven.—*Tr.*

SONG FOR A BARREL ORGAN

The refugees the bombers stopped
Turned and came back in broad daylight
Touched in the head, so tired they dropped
   Turned and came back in broad daylight
   Under their loads the women bent
   The men were crazy with their plight

Under their loads the women bent
And children crying for lost toys
Looked without knowing what it meant
   And children crying for lost toys
   Opened their eyes too wide upon
   The shattered world of little boys
Opened their eyes too wide upon
The bakery at the corner burned
The crossroads with a Hotchkiss gun

   At the corner where the bakery burned
   Soldiers who count in an undertone
   And a colonel looking unconcerned
The soldiers count in an undertone
Their dead and wounded one by one
From the schoolhouse comes a single groan
   The dead and wounded one by one
   Their girls at home, what will they do?
   Oh, sweetheart, if I were not gone

The girls at home, what will they do?
The men sleep with their photographs
The sky outlasts the swallows too
   The men sleep with their photographs
   On canvas stretchers head by head
   Each with a pictured girl who laughs

On canvas stretchers head by head
We'll take them away, the young men
Whose skin is gray, whose bellies red

    We'll take them away, the young men
    But who knows if it's worth our while
    Look, Sergeant, they'll be dead by then
And who knows if it's worth our while
Should they arrive at Saint-Omer
What will they find with every mile?
    Should they arrive at Saint-Omer
    The tanks have cut us from the sea
    They'll find the enemy is there

The tanks have cut us from the sea
We hear they've taken Abbeville
May all our sins forgiven be
    "We hear they've taken Abbeville"
    So said the gunners who passed by
    Seeing civilians at their heel
So said the gunners who passed by
Like painted ghosts, they were so pale
The wild head and the starting eye

    Like painted ghosts they were so pale
    A fellow who came into view
    Laughed like a savage at their tale
A fellow who came into view
He was as dark as the mines
As dark as life itself in hue
    He was as dark as the mines
    This giant going home again
    To Méricourt or Sallaumines

This giant going home again
Cried, "We return, no matter what
If it is bombs or only rain"

Cried, "We return no matter what
Better by far die where you are
With one or two shots in the gut
Better by far die where you are
Than go into a strange country
Better a hundred times in war

Die than go to a strange country.
We're turning back, we're going home
The heart full, the stomach empty
We're turning back, we're going home
All hope we lack and tears and arms
We found we're not allowed to roam
All hope we lack and tears and arms
Little they care in safety there
Those people chased us with gendarmes

Little they care in safety there
They sent us back beneath the bombs
'You can't get by,' they told us. 'Bear
Your lot. Go back beneath the bombs'
We're going while as yet we live
No need for us to dig our tombs
We're going while as yet we live
Still with our children, with our wives
Thanks to no one. No thanks we give"

Still with their children, with their wives
Saint Christophers of the hard road
They walked the way that cut like knives
Back to the flames, the burnt abode
Saint Christophers of the hard road
Giants outlined as they went by
No staff in hand to help the load
Giants outlined as they went by
Against the white rage of the sky.

*Translated, except for the title, by Sally Wood. She says in a foot-
note: "The title,* Complainte pour l'Orgue de la Nouvelle Barbarie,
*cannot be translated because we do not call a barrel organ an organ
of* Barbarie, *which can also mean barbarity. A* complainte *is a sad
popular song."*

RICHARD II FORTY

You may my glories and my state depose
But not my griefs. Still am I king of those.
Richard II, *Act IV, Scene I.*

My country is a bark adrift
Abandoned by her one-time crew
And I am not unlike that king
Left friendless when his luck turned ill
But monarch of his sorrows still

To live takes cunning now, no more
Winds cannot dry the tears I spill
Now must I hate what I adore
And what I lost must give away
While monarch of my sorrows still

The heart can almost cease to beat
The blood may run, though slow and chill
No longer two and two be four
When robbers play at blind man's buff
I am monarch of my sorrows still

Whether at sunset or at dawn
The skies are colorless and wan
Spring dies among the flower stalls
Bright Paris of my youth, farewell
I am monarch of my sorrows still

Forsake the fountains and the woods
Hide away, chattering birds, be still
Your songs are put in quarantine
The days have come when fowlers reign
I am monarch of my sorrows still

~ 39 ~

There is a time for suffering
Cut France in pieces if you will
When the Maid came to Vaucouleurs
The morning had this pallor too
I am monarch of my sorrows still.

Rolfe Humphries and Malcolm Cowley

THE UNOCCUPIED ZONE

Cross-fade of grief to nothingness,
The beat of the crushed heart grew less,
The coals grew white and lost their gleam;
Drinking the wine of summer's haze
In a rose-castle in Corrèze,
I changed this August into dream.

What could it be that of a sudden
Brought an aching sob in the garden,
A voice of low reproach in the air?
Ah not so soon, ah do not wake me;
This merest snatch of song must take me
Out of the barracks of despair.

I thought for a moment that I heard
In the middle of the corn a blurred
Noise of arms—a theme that sears.
Whence did this theme return to me?
Not carnations nor rosemary
Had thus retained the scent of tears.

By hook or crook I had got relief
From the dark secret of my grief
When lo—the shadows redivide;
My eyes were only on the track
Of apathy that looks not back
When September dawned outside.

My love, within your arms I lay
When someone hummed across the way
An ancient song of France; my illness
At last came clear to me for good—
That phrase of song like a naked foot
Rippled the green water of stillness.

Louis MacNeice

~ 41 ~

ELSA, I LOVE YOU

Beveled by every kiss
The years wear down too fast
Beware, beware of this
Sad breakage of the past

Oh, all one season how good it was to live
That summer was lovely as summer in a book
I was fool enough to think I was making you happy
When it was only the hills of the Grande Chartreuse
Or the spell of a sunset over Toulon harbor
Brief as the joy that in shadow wastes away

Beveled by every kiss
The years wear down too fast
Beware, beware of this
Sad breakage of the past

I sang farewell to the year when the leaves turned yellow
No matter, the exile believes in his return
And the dying man that a world is being born
Forgotten now are the words of the waltz we lived
But look in my eyes to find your beauty mirrored
Have you grown deaf to my folly, my self, my heart?

Beveled by every kiss
The years wear down too fast
Beware, beware of this
Sad breakage of the past

The sun repeats like that ash-pale pianist
Who sang a few words over, always the same
Chérie. . . . Remember those long unthreatened days
When the two of us lived together in Montparnasse?
Life will have flowed away and no one noticed
Colder. Evening already. The heart slows down

Beveled by every kiss
The years wear down too fast
Beware, beware of this
Sad breakage of the past

When I gave you those verses you liked their sentimental
Music, then put them away, like a four-leaf clover
They faded and died between my memory's pages
But once they pleased you and therefore I take them today
From out their forgotten cupboard as if I were singing
Elsa, I love you, my dear one, my wicked one

The years wear down too fast
Beveled by every kiss
Beware, beware of this
Sad breakage of the past

Glassy refrain with its murmuring monotone
It isn't for nothing ever that humming a tune
One says the words over and over again like spells
A day is coming when all the words are tears
Let us fasten tight the shutter that flaps unheard
This chorus comes down between us like drops of rain

Beware, beware of this
Sad breakage of the past
Beveled by every kiss
The years wear down too fast

Rolfe Humphries and Malcolm Cowley

NIGHTS

I. *Night in May*

The ghosts avoided the road where I went by
But mist in the pastures gave their breath away
Night poised in delicate grace above the plain
When we had left the walls of La Bassée

A farm on fire burns in the desert's heart
The weeds of the ditch feel silence crouching there
An airplane tells its beads and then lets fall
A rocket over Ablain Saint-Nazaire

The frightened ghosts swirl in confusion, lost
Among the hundred times repeated maze
The horizon knows the rising plumes of fear
Above the homes of Arras all ablaze

I see the interference of two wars
Here is the graveyard, here the hill appears
Night takes her orphaned sister by the hand
Our shadows join with those of other years

There in the grass they dream where no flag waves
Earth sunken, wooden cross without *Here lies*
The guides no longer lecture on their graves
Must they live again in our mythologies?

Blue ghosts of Vimy after twenty years
Half dead: I am the road of spiral dawn
Winding about the obelisk I know
Where the ill-slumbering, ill-buried go

General view of memory. Enough endured
It is finished. Rest. Which one of you cried No
At the guns' resuming noise? False Trianon
Real calvary, white crosses, grassy lawn

The dead resemble the living if they tremble
Asleep in bed, the living are the dead
Tonight the dead men tremble and resemble
The living, who are dead men disinterred

Was ever night so infinitely night?
But Musset and the Muses, where are they?
I can smell laburnum somewhere blooming bright
It is 1940. This is a night in May.

II. *Night at Dunkerque*

France underfoot like a worn-out carpet spread
Has shrunk away beneath our constant tread

We bivouac, a hundred thousand where
The beach of Malo bridges sea and air

And dead men drift like seaweed. Yachts and lighters
Are overturned to look like bishops' mitres

Into the air where rotting horseflesh reeks
Rises a sound as of stampeding beasts

The crossing gate lifts crooked arms to the sky
Within our breasts we feel the hearts awry

A hundred thousand hearts of landless men
When will they utter cries of love again?

O Saint Sebastians pierced, in agony
How much you are like me, how much like me

Alone will understand me the ill-starred
Who value more the heart's wound than the heart

But I shall cry this anguish, this desire
As night makes visible the flowers of fire

Shall cry aloud till sleepwalkers tumble down
From burning roofs all over the burning town

Shall cry my love like the man who used to screech
Knives, knives to grind, in the early-morning streets

Shall cry and cry, Where are you, eyes I love
Where have you flown, my lark, my mourning dove?

Louder than all the shells above me crying
Louder than drunkards, louder than the dying

Shall cry, Your lips are flagons where I find
The long draft of love that is like red wine

Your arms around me build a parapet
I cannot die. To die would be to forget

Seeing the eyes of the soldiers who embark
Who could forget his longing at Dunkerque?

Lying awake while star-shells flared and sank
Who could forget the potion that he drank?

Each soldier, having dug a life-size cave
Now sleeps as in the shadow of the grave

Faces like flint, demented attitudes
Over their slumber grim foreboding broods

Spring and its fragrance never haunt this land
Here May lies dying in the drifted sand.

III. *Night of Exile*

What does the exile care if the colors are false?
We put no trust in ghosts or apparitions
And yet, he says, I would swear that this was Paris
I can hear the violins tuning in the pit

The Opéra, he says, this fox-fire changing
I can see it now with my half-opened eyes
The glittering balconies, the silver fox
The sea-green roof like a dead emerald

I know, he says, those dancing girls of stone
Whose leader brandishes a tambourine
But how explain this underwater light?
The waking dreamer rubs his heavy eyes

Medusas, he says, and halos and half-moons
Unroll their pallor when I rub my eyes
In the Opéra hung with ropes of opal tears
Cellos and woodwinds orchestrate my sighs

I had meant to fix in my foolish memory
That pink, he says, that unknown lavender
That phantom mask at the end of the avenue
Changing her costume each night for us alone

Those nights, it hurts me to remember them
Had as many glints as the sloe-black eyes of doves
Nothing is left of those jewels in the darkness
And what night really is we know at last

Lovers have only love for an address
Seeing your eyes at sunset, I laid my bets
On a cyclamen-colored heaven over Paris
Nights hardly nights, color of tenderness

For you the heavens wagered all their diamonds
For you I played my heart on the even numbers
Whirling sun of the boulevards, pinwheels, rockets
How many stars in the streets and over the roofs

When I think back, I see the stars were cheating
The dreams were second-hand that flapped in the breeze
And the steps of the dreamers echoed on the pavement
While lovers embraced in the shade of the portes-cochères

Two of us peopled our arms' infinitude
Your whiteness set on fire the eternal gloom
I could not see in the shadow of your eyes
The golden eyes of the street that never went out

Do the vegetable wagons always lumber past?
Are they still drawn by lazy Percherons
Blue figures sleeping among the cauliflowers
And the horses of Marly rearing in the mist?

Do the milkmen hammer a false dawn out of tin
And, on their hooks outside the market booths
Do butchers hang fantastic carcasses
Pinning rosettes along the bloody sides?

Was it silenced for good one foggy afternoon
When tenderness had vanished into the twilight
The mechanical phonograph beneath our window
That for a penny sang its little tune?

Is that lost paradise forever gone
Concorde, the Halles, the Opéra, the Louvre?
Remember those nights as another night creeps down
The night that comes from the heart and has no dawn.

Rolfe Humphries and Malcolm Cowley

DEVILISH WEATHER

Devilish weather doing what it pleases
Being in Nice it thinks itself in Paris
And turns the Promenade des Anglais into
   A booby trap
There you meet a curious turn-out
Black marketeers trembling with cold
People stark naked looking for a king
   Pansies and tarts

Birdlike heads veering with every wind
Ready for anything. Hearts are trumps. For sale
Play the black. Get thee to a nunnery
   Or else to a theatre
Every remark sounds like an echo
The sea is the color of string beans
It is raining again on the Negresco
   Paler than plaster

Devilish weather not knowing what it wants
Snotty-nosed March using its handkerchief
No sooner rain than the sky turns blue again
   Like a thousand-franc bill
This brand-new shadow fastened to your steps
Whatever happened to make it disappear
Really you got no sort of price for it
   Poor Peter Schlemihl

Looking everywhere for a shadow to borrow
Exiled from walls and the common soil
Walking symbol of 1941
   Your pockets empty
Devilish weather putting his watch in hock
Not jealous when his wife is somewhere else
Claiming to have no fear of the wolf
   For the wolf is so friendly

Devilish weather. No joy without a coupon
Women wear hats like bonbons
Men send them ham-bones instead of flowers
    Laugh till they burst
Devilish weather when your dearest friends
Are enemies before you catch your breath
Black is white, the forbidden is allowed
    The best is the worst.

Rolfe Humphries

TEARS ARE ALIKE

In the gray sky were porcelain angels
In the gray sky were stifled cries
I remember those days at Mainz
The black Rhine and the weeping Loreleis

You would find sometimes at the end of an alley
A Frenchman dead with a knife-blade in the back
You would find sometimes that the peace was cruel
For all the young white wine of the terraces

I drank their transparent Kirschwasser
I drank the vows they whispered with clasped hand
How lovely were the palaces and churches
I was twenty then, I did not understand

What did I know about days of defeat
When your country is a love forbidden
When you need the voice of false prophets
To bring lost hope to life again?

I remember songs that touched the heart
I remember signs chalked in red
Found in the morning scribbled on walls
We never once deciphered what they said

Who can say where memory begins
Who can say where the present ends
Where the past becomes a sentimental ballad
And sorrow a paper yellowed with age?

Like a child surprised among his dreams
The blank looks of the vanquished made you start
Then, at the tramp of guard relieving guard
The Rhenish silence shuddered to its heart.

Rolfe Humphries and Malcolm Cowley

~ 51 ~

C

I have crossed the bridges of Cé [1]
It is there that everything began

A poem from out a time long past
Tells of a knight who injured lay

Of a rose upon the pavement cast
Of a bodice with an open stay

Of a mad duke's castle the poem tells
And of the swans in the castle moats

Of the meadow where dances every day
An everlasting fiancée

A song I have drunk like icy milk
Of glories long and falsely spun

The River Loire takes my thoughts away
With all the equipment overturned

And the guns untouched with safeties on
And the tears which run the tears which run

O France O my forsaken France
I have crossed the bridges of Cé.

William Jay Smith

[1] Les Ponts-de-Cé, the four "Caesar Bridges" near Angers, have
been the scene of repeated conflicts from the Roman period on. It
was to this point in 51 B.C. that the Gallic hero Dumnacus with-
drew in disastrous defeat before the Roman legions, much like the
French in 1940 before the German invaders.—*Tr.*

RICHARD COEUR-DE-LION

If the universe is like this gaol where now
At Tours in France we are as prisoners penned,
If strangers put our clover under plough
If day today is empty of an end

Must I mark up each hour upon a chart
As time to hate, who never had the will?
One has no home now—even in the heart,
O my country, are you my country still?

Not for me now to watch the swallow fly
Who speaks to heaven a language under ban
Nor watch the unreliable cloud go by,
Old ferryman of dreams that have had their span.

Not for me now to say what I am thinking
Nor hum this air that haunts my heart and brain;
I cannot face the silence without shrinking
And sunlight is as ill as fog or rain.

They are brute force and we are only legion;
You sufferers, we know where we belong.
Why make the night a yet more sombre region?
A prisoner can still compose a song

A song as pure as running water, white
As bread before the war, a song to rise
Above the manger clear into the night
And high enough to catch the shepherds' eyes

O all the shepherds, sailors, and Wise Men,
Carters and dons and butchers and the race
Of image-makers, tricksters with the pen,
And queues of women in the market-place

People in business and commercial roles
Men who make steel or textiles, also men
Whose job in life is scaling telegraph poles
And the black miners—all shall listen again

All Frenchmen are Blondel,[1] in each he sings:
Whatever name we called her at the start
Freedom—like a whispering of wings—
Answers the song of Richard Lionheart.

Louis MacNeice

[1] Blondel was a troubadour, the boon companion of Richard Coeur-de-Lion. There is a French legend that he wandered through Germany until he found the castle where Richard had been secretly imprisoned after his return from the Holy Land. To announce that help was near, he sang, outside the window, a ballad that Blondel and the king had written together.—M. C.

MORE BEAUTIFUL THAN TEARS

Some people cannot live whilst I'm alive,
I haunt their dreams with an untold remorse,
It seems my songs contain such bursts of brass
That even the dead must hear them in the grave.

Ah, if you wince at echoes in my work
Of clattering tanks, their grating springs' high squeal;
Know that the storm has drowned the organ's peal,
That I, for one, cannot forget Dunkerque.

Bad taste, I quite agree, but unlike you
Some of us saw hell mirrored in the sky,
And we shall not forget until we die
The cup we drained of Brussels' bitter brew.

You cannot stand the love of which I write,
I say it's fine, you say that it will rain;
My fields too white with daisies you complain,
My skies too blue by day, too full of stars by night.

You cry revenge, but is it not enough
That I whose simplest words you tear apart
And scrutinize, like a dissected heart,
Have lost for good the Louvre and the Pont-Neuf?

You may suppress a poet with your hate,
Pinion the wings that knew the joy of flight;
But in my love for France I have one right,
Do what you will, you cannot alienate.

Away, my beauty, ask from place to place
If I forget you or no longer care;
Your eyes are like the sheaf of flowers you bear
And buds of other springs your apron grace.

Was our love feigned, our passion a mere pose?
Look in her eyes how pensively she stares:
So I have sometimes seen a patch of tares
Set in relief the cornfields of La Beauce.

Are not her arms like those carved from the stone
Of villages where golden loaves are made?
Classic perfection that invokes the shade
Of Jean Racine at La Ferté-Milon.

The smile of Rheims upon her matchless face
Is like late sunshine in the summer air;
The smell of Champagne's presses in her hair
Would tempt the saints themselves to fall from grace.

Who could have traced but Ingres of Montauban
Her shoulder, where desire's impassioned kiss
May quench a thirst like theirs whose deepest bliss
Is water from pure mountain freshets drawn?

Would Petrarch not have loved, like Laura gone,
Her for whose injuries we bleed today?
Petrarch who flew, keen as a spear, to stay
The fawn that foiled the hunt at Avignon.

Call up again, to exorcise despair,
A mirage of those scenes I used to know,
From Vercors to the Pass of Roncevaux,
From Brantôme's vaults to Saint-Jean-du-Desert.

Northwards from Arles the wind blows memories
Of which my heart is yet too full to speak,
While the deep scars of hostile tanks still streak
The yellow swamps of Saintonge and Aunis.

O pageantry of province, town and stream,
Your flowerlike names challenge comparison:
Enthralled by legends of great lovers gone,
Our minds confound the vision with its theme.

Country of vines with grape-green pastures graced,
Alps that hem in the sky and the Durance,
Manosque, so dear to Francis, king of France,
That on its Saracen walls his name he traced.

Less dear than you are, wayward, jealous lover
Who cannot in my lines your image see:
Pause on Naurouze's watershed where we,
Linked by one fate, between two oceans hover.

But no, recurrent like an old refrain,
You must run on. After Mont Ventoux where?—
Look, there's the Seine once more, the orchards dear
To him who dreamed there of the Madeleine.

Landscape or woman, sleep-charmer, strong as wine,
Truly I know not which I paint, which love;
Nor if these golden thighs and breasts may prove
To be the westering pinewoods of Bretagne.

Breastplate of innocence, where I would taste
Joy's milk and cider and there rest replete:
For Normandy what conscript would not meet
An exile's death among Palmyra's dust?

I cannot tell you where her charms begin,
There are sensual place-names like Les Andelys;
But look this way now, and she weeps you see—
Ah Paris, Paris, do not cry in vain.

City of song and violent loyalties
Where every paving-stone's a barricade,
Stained flags now only in your laundries fade—
Paris, my Pole Star and Metropolis.

Heart of our grief, Paris of Cours-la-Reine,
Your white-robed nuns, your February skies;
Paris, more harrowing than the glaziers' cries
From the Faubourg St. Antoine to Suresnes.

Fly from these hideous suburbs where there are
No roots, but only what the next day brings;
None of the Oise or Marne now writes or sings,
And Sylvia haunts no more the desolate Valois.

Embattled memories, here long ago
Our young hearts yearned while heaven's foundations
    swam
Not for a woman's love, but the Chemin des Dames—
Traveler, recall the windmill at Laffaux.

Now honored dust beneath your footsteps stirs,
As eastwards still pursuing they are borne,
Seeking a deathless and dishonored dawn
Of glory in Argonne and by the Meuse.

As a fugitive will nurse the stricken roe,
The pond's blue eyes the gold-flecked brakes befriend:
Halt on the exile's road to Switzerland,
In Courbet's country where the mandrakes grow.

Alsace is lost, where when the Rhine's in flood
Bewildered pheasants from the branches fall,
And Werther at the peasants' Christmas ball
Forgets awhile the sorrows of his blood.

Shall the great storm that struck Dunkerque and then
Swept to Port-Vendre, all our loved voices quell?
None can destroy a legend, or expel
Aymon's boar-hunting sons from the Ardennes.

None can suppress that everlasting strain
Which, like a flute, through all our singing soars;
Cut though the laurels be, another cause
Claims the "Companions of La Marjolaine."

In the rose-leaves I hear the horseshoes drum:
Stop, runaway! Is it my full heart's beat?
(Hope's voice at night is like a fountain's, sweet)
Or just a horse? Or is Duguesclin come?

What matter if I die, it is enough
If others see that blessed face reborn:
Dance, children, dance your capucine, forlorn,
My country is Dearth, Penury, and Love.

John Hayward

I SALUTE YOU, MY FRANCE

I write in a land devastated by pest,
One would think a held-over nightmare of Goya,
Where the dogs have no hope save of heavenly feast,
And stooping white skeletons weed the soya.

A land overrun by a merciless gang
Whipping cattle from pastures and pigs from their sties,
A country disputed by claw and fang,
Calamitous days under pitiless skies.

Under the heel of the puppet mutter
Lands cleft in ruts to the heart from their wheels;
Marked for rotated cutting by King Guttersputter. . . .
A white land of fear where the werewolf steals.

I write in a country where men are pastured
In filth and in thirst, in hunger and silence. . . .
Where the son is snatched from the mother and quar-
    tered,
As if Herod reigned, with Laval for crown-prince!

I write in this country disfigured by blood,
A midden-mound, now, of wounds and of groans,
An open market that hail and rain flood,
A ruin where death plays at knuckle-bones.

I write in this country where the police
Enter the dwellings at all hours and seasons;
And inquisitors, driving in splinters, won't cease
To scrutinize broken limbs, searching for treasons.

I write in this country of a thousand deaths,
And purple wounds from the pack that harry
Her, swarming upon her with reeking breaths,
While the huntsmen's trumpet sounds the quarry!

I write in this land that the butchers flay,
Leaving nerves and entrails and bones laid bare;
Where the forests are torches burnt away,
And fleeing the wheat on fire, birds in the air. . . .

I write in this night, deep and criminal,
Where I hear the breathing of foreign soldiers. . . .
And the trains strangling in the distant tunnel
From which, if they issue, God alone knows!

I write on a tilting-field of ill-mated
Opponents: one with war-horse and armor;
And the other exposed to the sword, lacerated,
Has solely for armor his right and his valor!

I write in this den, where not simply a prophet,
But a nation, is thrown to the jaws of the beasts,
And is summoned to never forget its defeat
But to give to the bears the flesh due their feasts.

I write on this tragic stage where the actors
Have lost their way, and wander, faint,
In the hollow theatre where the malefactors
Mouth ponderous words for the ignorant.

I write in this great convict-settlement. . . .
In a dungeon, at night, alive with vibrations
Of messages rapped on the walls and sent,
Inflicting on the jailers strange hallucinations!

How should I speak to you of flowers
And utter no cries in all I write?
I see but three colors in rainbow-showers;
You have banned the songs that gave me delight. . . .

If I could skim earth of its evil dreams
And the shadows of monsters that lie over it,
Find Paradise lost with its four silver streams,
And freshen my song as I fly over it!

I say with words mechanical things
More mechanically than falling snow;
Demonetized words like the paper brings—
The language that the people know.

Like a penny dropping on the asphalt
That makes us turn in the midst of our walk,
At the echo of tragic misfortune we halt
As a word's dropped by chance—one not used in talk!

There's a hope of double-sense in our French words,
Like the meadow remembering a morning-shower;
They vibrate long in their determined chords,
And the simplest among them have greatest power.

Whether of birds and metamorphoses,
Of August fading in the honey-clover,
Whether I sing of roses or the breeze,
My music breaks into sobs, over and over.

The fields are barren when my people groan;
There burns in the eyes a troubled amnesia
Of poetry. . . . There's a scent of brimstone
In the air, resembling the mines of Silesia.

It seems absurd to set in rhymes
Facts so well known, though to state them is treason;
Is it giving wings, say, to their crimes
To describe in French verse a German prison?

If I write, it's to furnish hate a bell
To accent the lessons of inhuman wrong:
On the confines of Poland, exists a hell
Whose name shrieks and whistles a grisly song.

Ausschwitz! Ausschwitz! O bleeding syllables!
In its slow fires one lives, one perishes
In leisured execution, as the pulse
Indicates how the heart little by little dies.

Limits of hunger, limits of force:
The road of even the Christ was not worse,
Nor the interminable searing divorce
Of the soul from the inhuman universe.

Olympics of suffering are held in this place
Where death is in pitiless combat with fear;
We have our French team in this frightful race,
And a hundred of our women are here.

There are a hundred fleurons of the halo
That crown with blood this bitter country, sated
With the hundred teachings of the school of Nero
Where we have learned the love of having hated!

Since to say them now is not in my power—
The hundred names sons, husbands, brothers carry
In their hearts, I salute you in this fearful hour,
Mary-Claude, saying: I salute you, Mary. . . .

And the one who went first out into the night,
As rises to Liberty the first pure cry,
Mary-Louise Fleury, returned to the light
Beyond the tomb: I salute you, Mary. . . .

Alas, their sowings glisten
With blood this long summer! we say
It lasts overlong: listen,
They took Danièle and Maïe. . . .
Will they strip the petals, one by one,
From our sweet France torn away?

The shadows deepen like a knell
On fields with misery wrung,
And words are powerless to reveal—
Maïe and Danièle. . . . Is it possible?
How can one finish the terrible tale
That stifles the heart and the song?

I salute you, Marys of France, of a hundred faces,
And those of you who timeless glory wear
Unatonable to assassins of hostages,
Simply surviving those that they loved there!

And those among you for whom men are waiting,
Trembling to think what may be your fate,
Fearing to recover only your legend,
Bending beneath the terrible weight. . . .

They thought they had touched the nadir of absence:
They doubted fate held a worse cruelty.
For them, your return will be a renascence. . . .
How put back a heart that's been taken away?

But even in love, birth is always pain. . . .
What tales will you tell in the arms of your men?
They think of it nights, they dream of it days. . . .
Let you smile and their lives start over again.

When you return, for return you will,
There will be flowers for which you yearn. . . .
Of roses and lilies you'll have your fill. . . .
There will be flowers when you return!

You will awaken in transparent dawnings,
And the children will come to kiss your martyred hands;
Your tired feet will tread on moss, and mornings
Of music and repose will loose your bands.

The gardens breathing when the night is borning. . . .
Leafage of summer, verdure of the prairie!
The swallow just now on my window-sill in the dawning
Saying, it seemed to me: I salute you, Mary!

I salute you, my France, snatched from the ghosts! at
    home!
Restored to peace! ship saved from the hurricane!
I hear you sing: Orléans, Beaugency, Vendôme!
Bells, bells, sound the angelus of the birds again!

I salute you, my France, with eyes of the turtle-dove,
Never too much my torment, too much my love!
My France, my new and my eternal theme,
Soil sown with heroes, birds in the sky like a dream. . . .

I salute you, my France, where winds become calm!
My France of forever, whose geography
Extends in the sea-breeze its open palm
For the bird of the air to alight trustingly!

I salute you, my France, where the bird in migration
From Lille to Roncevaux, from Mont-Cenis to Brest,
For first time has learned the apprenticeship lesson
Of what it may cost to abandon a nest!

Country impartial to dove or to eagle,
Of song and of valor the double habitation!
My France, I salute you where wheat stands regal
In ripening ranks of richest variation. . . .

I salute you, my France, where the people are clever
In works that make the days a delight;
They will come from afar to salute you forever,
Paris, my heart, survivor of night!

Happy and strong at last, your shoulders wrapped
In rainbow-promise flood will not pollute
Again the fields where Liberty has stepped,
My France beyond the deluge, I salute!

Grace Wallace

~ 65 ~

ELSA AT THE MIRROR

It was in the middle of our tragedy
And all the long day sitting at her glass
She combed her bright gold hair. To me it was
As though her calm hands quieted a blaze.
It was in the middle of our tragic days.

And all day long sitting before her glass
She combed her bright gold hair as one who plays
In the very middle of our tragedy
A golden harp without belief, to pass
The long hours, sitting all day at her glass.

She combed her bright gold hair and seemed to be
Martyrizing at will her memory
All the long day while sitting at her glass,
Reviving still the spent flowers of the blaze,
Not speaking as would another in her place.

She martyrized at will her memory
It was in the middle of our tragic days
Her dark glass was the world's facsimile
Her comb, parting the fires of that silken mass,
Lit up the corners of my memory.

In the very middle of our tragic days
As Thursday is in the middle of the week

And sitting there before her memory
She saw within the glass (but did not speak)

One by one the actors of our tragedy
Dying, whom most in this dark world we praise

I need not call their names You know what memory
Burns on the hearth of these declining days

And in her golden hair when she sits there
And combs in silence the reflected blaze.

George Dillon

BALLAD OF ONE WHO SANG AT THE STAKE

". . . If it had to be done all over
   I would take this road again."
The voice that sang tomorrow's song
   Rose from the iron chains.

Two men, they say, came into his cell,
   Came stealing in that night.
They said to him, "Give in, give in,
   Are you tired of life and light?

Only a word and you can live,
   One word will set you free;
Say but a word and you can live,
   Like us, on bended knee."

". . . If it had to be done all over
   I would take this road again."
The voice that sang tomorrow's song
   Rose from the iron chains.

"Only a word! Your troubles end,
   The door swings wide and free,
The torturer puts his tools away.
   Say, *Open sesame!*

Only a word, only a lie,
   To change your destiny.
Recall, reflect, remember long
   How sweet the mornings be."

". . . If it had to be done all over
   I would take this road again."
The voice that sang the song in chains
   Spoke for tomorrow's men.

"I know the story. A lion dead
  Is less than a living ass;
I remember what good King Henry said,
  That Paris is worth a mass,

But not for me ever." Let them go.
  Let his blood be on his head.
He has thrown his only chance away.
  The fool is as good as dead.

If it had to be done all over
  Would he take this road again?
"I would do it tomorrow," sang the voice
  That rose from the iron chains.

"I die and I leave my only love,
  My France that will never die;
I go to my death, and O my friends
  You will know the reason why."

In the gray morning the jailers came,
  Speaking their German tongue.
Someone translated, "Will you give in?"
  But firmly the answer rung:

". . . If it had to be done all over
  I would take this road again.
The song of tomorrow will rise above
  The sound of your leaden rain."

At the stake he was singing the Marseillaise,
  "The bloodstained banners wave."
It took a second volley of lead
  To keep him from ending the stave.

Another song rose to his lips,
  French as the song replaced,
Yet chanted as a Marseillaise
  For all the human race.

                    Rolfe Humphries

CHRISTMAS ROSES

When we were the wineglass overturned,
Were the cherry tree of blossom shorn,
The broken crust, the plowland upchurned
And the drowned through Paris riverborne;

When we were the yellow trampled grass,
The pilfered granary, the loose shutter,
The song choked off, the sob from the mass,
The fallen horse that pants in the gutter;

When we were exiles in our own France
Who wandered the highroads begging alms,
To spectres holding in suppliance
The pitiful bareness of our palms,

Then, then was the moment they uprose,
If briefly, if in a day struck down—
In dead of winter blossomed the rose,
The gleam of swordblades was in their frown.

Noel, Noel! That faint sunrise
Gave back to you, men of little faith,
The love for which one willingly dies
And the future that relives his death.

Dare you take the road December went,
Bright Aprils beyond the years of dread,
Or dare recall the roses' deep scent
With the shepherds' planet overhead?

At morning will you forget the star
And the dawn forget at eventide,
Or sailing with godsent winds deplore
The altar on which the victims died?

And if, on the Easter daisy's wax,
Blood against pallor, a blush should rise,
Will you forget the always waiting axe?
Will you look back at them with absent eyes?

Spilt blood cannot forever be still.
Will you forget what nourished the grain,
And the grape-red lips against the soil
And the black taste the vintages retain?

Helen Burlin and Malcolm Cowley

PARIS

Where there is good in the storm's heart of rage
Where in the heart of the night it is fair
The air is alcohol and misfortune courage
Windowframes broken hope still glimmers there
And from ruined walls the songs climb the air.

Never extinguished reborn from its blaze
Eternal glow of our motherland this
From Point du Jour until Père Lachaise
In August most sweet reflorescent of rose trees
Folk of everywhere the blood of Paris.

There's no éclat like Paris this dust under
Nothing so pure as her brow's resurgent wave
Nothing is so strong not fire nor thunder
As my Paris her dangers defiant to outbrave
Nothing so lovely as this Paris I have.

Nothing before made my heart to beat thus
Nothing my laughter with my tears so mated
As this cry of my people victorious
Nothing is so vast as a shroud torn and shed
Paris, Paris, of herself liberated.

Stephen Spender

PROSE

ARAGON: RESISTANCE LEADER

AMERICAN soldiers who hit the beaches of the Riviera in the middle of August 1944, were astonished at the thorough organization of French resistance forces. The expert coöperation of the French resistance with Allied liberation armies made possible the swift campaign through the Alps and up the Rhône Valley to Alsace in one blazing month.

We had been in constant liaison with the resistance movement, and we were aware of many of their courageous actions against their German conquerors. Some help had been expected, but not a fraction of the bold offensive moves that sped our advance. We found an even more intricate organization than we had believed possible under the dangerous conditions of clandestine struggle.

This was true, not only of military and intelligence organization, but even more of the organization of all phases of civil life. Those of us who were responsible for helping the French reëstablish their own organs of public information were struck by the advance arrangements for immediate output of all types of reading matter. In each town we found editors and supporting staffs at their posts, ready to issue their first official newspapers within a few hours of the liberation.

They were ready because they had been editing clandestine newspapers for more than three years under Vichy and German-occupation control, when death or deportation was the price paid by those who were caught. They knew how to produce a newspaper under any circumstances, and how enthusiastically they went about their work when they were free!

In Grenoble, heart of the Alpine maquis area, we found a group of newspaper men all set to go to work, with André Rousseaux, Catholic literary critic of the newspaper *Figaro*, in charge. It was he who first told us how French writers and intellectuals, headed by Louis Aragon, had gathered in the region of Dieulefit (God-made-it), a little Protestant town in the mountains of the Drôme department.

Aragon, he said, had been in constant touch with the newspaper men, and, as head of the National Writers' Committee in the southern zone of France, had directed the work of clandestine publication and helped select the men who would take over on the day of liberation. Local editors throughout the area also told us of the help Aragon had given them in assembling staffs, arranging for the seizure of printing plants so that the Germans would not destroy them in their retreat, and the hiding of paper stocks so that publication could be resumed immediately on their departure.

At this time the mountain area between the Isère and the Rhône River valley had just been liberated after the battle of Montélimar, when American troops sweeping through the Alps cut to pieces three German divisions retreating from Marseilles. Our forward troops were still fighting their way into Lyons. It was hard to find any of the newspaper editors or writers who knew the exact whereabouts of Aragon. He was in the liberated area, that was all they knew.

Aragon was still the elusive character he had been during the clandestine period. But everyone assured us that he was alive and very active. All had seen him at one time or another during the underground struggle. He had personally appeared at a friend's house, or at a certain restaurant for a quiet dinner, to discuss some important pamphlet that must be written, printed, and distributed to expose the latest atrocities of the Germans and the Vichy militia. Many of these men had edited underground newspapers, assigning articles to writers they never saw, confident that the work would be done and delivered to printers they did not know. Aragon had communicated some of his own personal fire and warmth and determination to each of these men.

All of them, from Catholics to Communists, had a tremendous respect for Aragon. They knew him, not only for his poems which had made him the voice of French resistance at home as well as abroad, but as the man who had helped give them confidence again in their own work and who had helped to solve many of their problems. They explained how he had used the National Writers' Committee to bring together lawyers, doctors, nurses, journalists, and magistrates into other active professional groups serving the resistance movement.

One day we were sent on a long mission across the wild mountains of the area, through the Vercors and the Drôme to Dieulefit to fetch some more writers needed by Rousseaux for the operation of Radio Grenoble, one of the first French radio stations back on the air after the liberation. At Dieulefit they told us that we could find Aragon and his wife, Elsa Triolet, in the little village of St. Donat, waiting to move into Lyons as soon as our troops broke in. We also learned their pseudonyms and obtained directions to their house.

From Dieulefit we drove for hours through one of those sudden mountain thunderstorms that sweep down from the Alps. It was icy cold in the open jeep, with its narrow canvas roof, and gusts of wind lashed us with freezing rain and sleet. The rain had stopped, and a bright red sun on the horizon lit up the streamers of storm cloud sweeping over the wild mountains as we climbed the hills from Romans to St. Donat.

Louis Aragon and Elsa Triolet were just putting the latest edition of their liberation newspaper, *La Drôme en Armes*, to bed as we arrived. We were welcomed in their tiny downstairs living room. "Elsa," Louis shouted up the narrow, steep stairs, "stop working on the paper and hurry down. We've got a new story! Look who's here!" Elsa almost fell into our arms in her haste.

We sat talking for hours, shivering at first from the cold, until we grew warm inside out from the hot, raw marc which Aragon passed out liberally for the great occasion. "We made it ourselves last autumn," he boasted. "We have no coal, and wood is now hard to get. I'm sorry we can't offer you a fire to dry yourselves. But you can kill that chill with this."

The first thing Aragon started talking about was the state of mind of his people. With eloquent gestures, with the haste of a man who had wanted to say these things to someone from America for a long time, he poured out a flood of words. He warned us of the relics of Nazi propaganda still left in the minds of many people, of the raw sensibilities created by years of oppression.

"We have suffered a great deal," he said, "but especially spiritually. You cannot know what it means to live each day without knowing what the morrow will bring. Whether your loved ones, your people, or even you yourself may disappear next. To see those you know, respect, and love vanish, to learn only months later that they have been shot or deported to an even worse fate in some distant slave camp in Germany. To know that each word, each thought, each act on behalf of your country, each protest for freedom of expression might be your passport to another world. To see the strength of your people oozing away, sapped deliberately, viciously, physically and morally, by a cunning enemy who knows how to measure the importance of the mind, who has skillfully studied how to poison it. To watch this poison distilled by his vast propaganda machine injected into the minds of simple men and women everywhere, and to watch the gnawing effect of doubt and fear and suspicion on those brave enough to fight back. You cannot know what these things mean. You had to live here to understand them.

"Don't forget to treat our people as tried and trusted

allies. To forget these things would leave us disillusioned, would crack our morale and courage, already strained by privation, tension, waiting, and misery. Tell the Americans whom you know, with whom you work, to respect what France has done. Help her in her hard task of regaining strength and confidence. Grant her the equality among peoples she has earned by her struggle."

It was an impassioned plea, a poetic plea. We heard it many times, often more haltingly expressed. No one begged for our understanding; they claimed it as a right.

And that afternoon we began to hear from Aragon's own lips, in answer to the many questions we fired at him, the first details of those four years of struggle against the German attempt to crush the spirit of the French people. It was a struggle in which he himself had played an important role from the day he left his newspaper desk to answer the mobilization call in August 1939. Many of the details were later filled in for me by colleagues who had worked with Aragon at various times. Aside from his organizational activities, his literary output during the four occupation years was stupendous. And when one considers the conditions under which he was forced to live and work, hunted both by the Nazis and the French fascist militia, his story seems even more incredible.

* * *

The very day of the armistice, June 25, a telegram from Elsa Triolet reached Aragon from Bordeaux. It had been sent June 13, and since then the Germans had occupied Bordeaux. Aragon nevertheless telegraphed back and a few days later his wife joined him by car at Javerlhac, in the Dordogne, where his division had withdrawn with the first ratification of the demarcation line. She lived with him at headquarters until he was demobilized on July 31.

Now it was time to begin all over again, but with Elsa beside him, Aragon felt that more than half the fight was won. They went to the château of Renaud de Jouvenel in the Corrèze Department, where they remained for three weeks while Aragon hunted up civilian clothes and found out that Gallimard, his French publisher, was in Carcassonne. One could not camp on friends indefinitely, so they visited the publisher to see what he could do for them. Business was too uncertain, said Gallimard. He could advance no money for the moment, he could settle no pending accounts. Aragon then sent a cable to his friend and publisher in America, Samuel Sloan, who answered promptly, sending him the funds to carry them until more could be earned.

In Carcassonne the Aragons often visited the poet Joë Bousquet, paralyzed as a result of wounds in the last war. Scores of writers, artists, poets, intellectuals of all kinds crowded into Bousquet's dim, shuttered room and talked in cautious tones of what had happened and what was to come. There came Jean Paulhan and his wife, Julien Benda, Jean Schlumberger, Boris Wilde, one of the first scientists to fall before the Nazi firing squads after the "Musée de l'Homme" arrests the following year. Even men of doubtful and dangerous views passed through, such as Jean Mistler, one of Pétain's emissaries in the last days of the Republic, for Bousquet's door was closed to none.

The Aragons remained in Carcassonne from the end of August until the end of December, renting rooms in the home of an old woman who had once owned a grocery store, a fervid admirer of Marshal Pétain. There Louis continued writing the poems for Le Crève-Coeur, and waiting for money. Their landlady, touched by their plight, and unaware of their political sympathies, offered to buy another shop which they could run for her. The business promised them a livelihood in the hard times to come, and besides they could always eat their stock in case of need, but the Aragons resisted the temptation. The police hounded them and only Aragon's recent war decorations saved him from arrest.

He went on writing, showing his poems to his friends, sometimes reading them in Bousquet's house. Even his friends were scandalized. This was too dangerous. It was asking for trouble. Aragon argued with them. To them patriotism at such a moment required them to be silent. But to Aragon, silence would indicate only prudence, or rather cowardice. It was necessary for poets, he insisted, to invent new ways of expressing themselves, not to be dumb.

But he was almost alone in thinking and acting thus. His position in Carcassonne was further endangered when *Le Figaro*, published in Lyons after the armistice, obtained one of his most powerful poems of this period, "Les Lilas et les Roses," and published it without his permission. Various friends warned him not to allow the publication of such outspoken thoughts. Men who later joined the struggle with Aragon still had confidence in the Marshal at that time.

The first fruitful visit Aragon had was from Pierre Seghers and his wife, who came from Villeneuve-les-Avignon to see him. After the armistice Seghers had revived his war-time review *Poètes Casqués,* as *Poésie 40.* It was the first time the two men had met. Seghers begged Aragon to help him keep the young review alive and to use it as a medium for an independent group of writers.

Only a short time before Aragon had received a letter from a friend in Morocco, giving him details of the death of the old French poet, Saint-Pol Roux. Nazi soldiers, running amok after their swift conquest of France, had broken into the grounds of his Villa Coecelian, and attacked his daugher, Divine. They raped the young woman and the family servant who ran to help her. When the aged poet tried to intervene, they beat him and the maid with their rifle butts. Both Roux and the faithful servant died within a few days, the old man more from a broken heart than from his wounds.

Seghers, seeing how deeply Aragon was moved by

this incident, so contrary to the "correct" attitude that was then being played up by both German and Vichy propaganda in France, asked him to write an article on Roux for *Poésie*. Seghers has described how Aragon sat down and in one hour wrote a magnificent defense of the French spirit in the moment of defeat. "Saint-Pol Roux, ou l'Espoir" was published under Aragon's own name with extensive cuts by the Vichy censors, in one of the first numbers of *Poésie*.

Aragon completed the poems for *Le Crève-Coeur* in September 1940 at Carcassonne. Not until late that winter was he able to deliver the text and discuss publication with Jean Paulhan, who came to visit him in Nice. Paulhan brought the manuscript back to Paris with him, and induced Gallimard, Aragon's publisher, to print it in the spring of 1941. Gallimard's hesitation was overcome when he saw that *Le Figaro* had not been molested by the Germans for publishing "Les Lilas et les Roses."

Towards the end of December 1940 the Aragons were able to move from their lodgings in Carcassonne. They accepted an invitation from the Seghers to visit them at their home in the village of Les Angles, near Villeneuve-les-Avignon, at Christmas time. The Seghers pressed them to stay and live with them, but the winter was bitter, and the house impossible to heat, so the Aragons decided to move on to Nice. Seghers again asked Aragon to become editor of *Poésie*, but he refused because his well-known political opinions might compromise the usefulness of the review. The two poets decided, at a time when hardly anyone dared publicly to voice his opinions, to reunite those writers who had not betrayed their country. At that time almost no writer, even the contributors to *Poésie*, thought of attacking the Germans, few having any clear idea of what was possible. Aragon and Seghers planned by letters and personal influence, by the example of the magazine itself, to arouse the conscience of young literary men and to demonstrate how they could express themselves despite the Vichy censorship. As part of this program Aragon also wrote his article "La Leçon de Riberac," summarizing his own reactions when he first heard of the armistice.

Poésie was thus the first legal literary review of the resistance writers. To those who still may feel that all authorized literature produced under the Vichy regime was emasculated and inept, I would recommend a thorough reading of the nineteen numbers of *Poésie* published during the occupation. The first numbers after the defeat opened with the moving stanzas of *Le Crève-Coeur,* and included articles and poems by Loys Masson, Pierre Emanuel, Louis Parrot, and others. Persistent pressure on the new censorship department had won a license for the new publication, and the collaborationist and German censors either did not scan its pages too closely, or were singularly thick-skulled and could not understand all its pointed barbs.

After several days with Seghers the Aragons moved on to Nice, where they arrived the evening of December 31, 1940. They were to live constantly on the Riviera, except for innumerable trips throughout the country, from January 1, 1941 until November 11, 1942.

Having decided that his duty during the occupation was to help the writers to play their part in the resistance movement, Aragon lost no time in setting to work. One of his outlets was provided by Max-Pol Fouchet, who had gone to North Africa just before the armistice and had founded one of the outstanding legal literary reviews of unoccupied France, *Fontaine*. In the following months Fouchet received and published in *Fontaine* a number of poems from *Le Crève-Coeur,* the article "La Leçon de Riberac" and a short story by Elsa Triolet.

An important development at this time was the foundation, at Geneva, of the review and publishing house called the *Cahiers du Rhône,* which published a more complete collection of French resistance literature during the war than any other publisher in the world. In the spring of 1941 Aragon wrote to Geneva to the well-known Swiss literary critic, Albert Béguin, asking if he would help French writers evade the censorship. They had known each other since 1920, when Béguin, then a student, traveled to Paris to meet the young Dadaist Aragon. Béguin replied promptly, offering to assist wholeheartedly. Shortly thereafter, he sent a friend, Bernard Arthonioz, to Nice to see Aragon, and after long discussions, in which Aragon made it clear that many French writers would break their silence if they were sure of an independent publication, the *Cahiers du Rhône* was founded in Geneva.

In addition to this work both Louis Aragon and Elsa Triolet resumed their writing in Nice. They were settled in a modest pension on a quiet street. Here Aragon completed the collection of poems which were sent to Switzerland and brought out there under the title of *Les Yeux d'Elsa* late in 1941. Elsa continued work on her short novels which were later published as *Mille Regrets*.

* * *

In June 1941 they decided that it was important for them to go to Paris to establish closer liaison with the writers in the north. Although it was now possible for persons who lived in Paris to return to their homes, the Aragons felt that it would not be safe for them to ask for official documents, and they arranged to cross the demarcation line by stealth. Georges Dudach, who had helped bring out a number of clandestine reviews in Paris in the months after defeat, and who was later to be shot by the Germans, was sent by the French Communist Party to guide them through. Crossing the demarcation line on foot, south of Tours, they were picked up by a German patrol and interned with hundreds of others who had been caught in the same fix. They carried their own identification papers, but the fame of Louis Aragon had not reached the Germans at that time. "A good lesson in modesty," said Aragon. They were released on July 16, and proceeded on their way to Paris.

In Paris Aragon saw a number of his friends, including Georges Politzer, Jacques Decour, Jean Paulhan, Georges Duhamel, Danièle Casanova, and others. Up to that time the only serious resistance review in Paris was the philosophic review *La Pensée Libre*, founded by Politzer and Jacques Decour. Only one number had appeared thus far but it had had a powerful effect in stimulating many intellectuals in Paris to take an active role in resistance work. The writers gathered at an informal meeting at which it was decided to establish a National Writers' Committee, and to begin publication of a clandestine review. In addition to those mentioned above, François Mauriac, the Dominican priest Reverend Père Meydieu, Jean Blanzat and Jean Guéhenno were present at this first meeting. Jacques Decour was named secretary of the group.

July 1941 was a tense period in Paris, and after accomplishing their main objectives the Aragons were advised to return to the south. They went via southwestern France, first visiting Renaud de Jouvenel at Castel Novel, where the Moussinacs joined them. Passing by Cahors to see his mother, Aragon by chance met a young artist friend, Boris Taslitzky, who was working at the Aubusson tapestry center with a group of leading French artists, including Jean Lurçat, Gromaire and Dufy.

The revival of the art of French tapestry weaving at Aubusson at the most sombre period of the defeat was analogous to the revival of poetry under the stimulus of Seghers and Aragon. Aragon suggested that they adopt the old French method of using poetry as a border legend in weaving their tapestry, as had been done in the 15th century. The idea was taken up with enthusiasm and in full occupation some of the most beautiful modern tapestries sold in France carried the verses of Eluard, Aragon, Apollinaire and others. The artists themselves began writing their own poetry, which they later printed in a regional review, *Les Etoiles de Quercy*.

From Cahors the Aragons went on to visit Seghers at

Les Angles. En route, they stopped off at Toulouse to see Georges Sadoul, and through him made contact with Jean Cassou, who was arrested shortly thereafter. While in prison Cassou wrote the beautiful poems later published as 33 *Sonnets Composés au Secret.*

Seghers had made considerable progress with *Poésie,* but pro-German collaborationists were still making headway among the intellectuals in the south. Drieu La Rochelle had become editor of the *Nouvelle Revue Française* and was making strenuous efforts to persuade French intellectuals to accept the "new order." He had sent his friend, René Vincent, to Vichy, to start a collaborationist review under the title of *Idées.* In 1942 Vincent showed his true colors by accepting the post of chief of censorship under Pétain. In Toulouse another literary review had been started by a group of Pétainist writers, aided by a number of Gestapo agents, called *Pyrénées.* While neither of these gained much prestige, they were causing confusion in some circles, and there was always the danger that they might grow more influential in time.

To counterbalance these, *Poésie,* and in North Africa *Fontaine,* were now on the right track. There were a number of other innocuous reviews in existence. *Les Cahiers du Sud* appeared in Marseilles, edited tactfully but honestly. In Lyons a clever rogue passed himself off to a group of intellectuals, sons of rich local industrialists, as a representative of Cardinal Gerlier, Archbishop of Lyons, and in the spring of 1941 induced them to put up the money for a fairly mediocre review, *Confluences.* There were, however, two reliable young men on the staff of *Confluences,* both of whom had talent. One was René Tavernier, son of a leading silk manufacturer; the other Marc Barbezat.

Barbezat recently had initiated a review of his own, called *L'Arbalète,* which contained much work by British, Russian and American authors hitherto untranslated. It was hand-printed by Barbezat himself on excellent paper in limited editions of only 400 copies twice a year. *L'Arbalète* set a high standard for this period.

In Lyons there were also the literary section of *Figaro*, edited by the Catholic writer and critic, André Rousseaux; a weekly short-story magazine, *Sept Jours*, edited by Louis-Martin Chauffier and staffed by a sound and energetic group of young writers; and a number of newspapers on which various literary men from Paris had found employment.

Aragon decided to visit the writers in the Lyons area and win their coöperation. In Lyons he met Andrée Viollis, one of the leading French women journalists, Edith Thomas, who was just beginning to show her great powers as a short story writer, André Rousseaux, Marc Barbezat, Stefan Priacel, Claude Aveline, Louis-Martin Chauffier, and two former friends who were now active resistance workers, Georges Altman and Pascal Pia, whom he persuaded to join in the work of the Writers' Committee.

Returning to Villeneuve-les-Avignon, the Aragons were put up at the home of Seghers' mother-in-law. Their visit was well-timed. It coincided with the opening of a congress of young intellectuals called *Jeune France*, at the Château de Lourmarin near Avignon. Although it was sponsored by Vichy, many young patriots already belonged to this organization and some of its leaders, like Claude Roy, later became very active in the resistance movement. Artists, musicians, poets, actors and writers were invited to the congress, and an invitation was even extended to Aragon himself. He decided not to go, but encouraged many of his friends to attend, and to use this screen to create an organization of patriot artists and writers. Among those present was Max-Pol Fouchet, who had made the trip from Algiers for this purpose and to consult with his friends at *Poésie*.

In fact, the *Jeune France* congress was paralleled by a series of meetings at Avignon and Villeneuve, where the writers and intellectuals spoke openly among themselves and began to formulate concrete plans for the future. Immediately upon his return from Paris in July, Aragon had written the first manifesto to resistance writers, and at these meetings he circulated it widely. Fouchet took a copy of it back to North Africa with him. It was decided that Loys Masson should move in with Seghers and assist as co-editor, and that every effort should be made to win over other reviews then being published.

Another important visitor at Villeneuve was Albert Béguin, who came with his wife, Raymonde Vincent, also a writer, to pick up some manuscripts for publication in Switzerland and to establish a more regular liaison than had existed heretofore. It was arranged that contact would be maintained through the new Swiss consul at Lyons, François Lachenal. Lachenal placed himself at the disposal of the resistance writers and was of invaluable aid. The books and reviews published by the *Cahiers du Rhône* and other publishers in Switzerland flowed back into France in considerable quantity through the connivance of the French censor at Annemasse on the Swiss frontier. He was an active member of the resistance movement and later joined the maquis in the Upper Savoy when he fell under suspicion. It was typical of the period that one of the most widely circulated reviews in France at the time was a Swiss weekly, called *Curieux*. The review was a hodgepodge of ideas, but it was possible to slip into its pages a considerable quantity of patriotic literature.

* * *

In October 1941 the Aragons returned to Nice. At Villeneuve and upon their return to Nice, Elsa completed the stories for *Mille Regrets*. It was an immediate success when published in Paris by Denoël in May 1942.

The autumn and winter of 1941 were a dangerous period for French writers in general, and for the Aragons in particular. To begin with, their landlady threw them out of her pension. They were not to learn until much later that the real reason was that in their absence the police had come and insisted that she report regularly on their activities, which the good woman would not do. Nor did she dare refuse the police; so she did the next best thing. The Aragons found a small apartment on the Quai des Etats-Unis, and despite the intense cold and the shortage of food, continued their work undisturbed.

With the appearance in Paris of Aragon's *Le Crève-Coeur* shortly after his return to the south there was a vicious outcry from the collaborationist writers. In the October number of the *Nouvelle Revue Française* Drieu la Rochelle accused Aragon of being the leading organizer of all resistance writers in France, author of many attacks against the Germans and Vichy and director of the clandestine press network. All of which was flattering but not quite true. There were others in the conspiracy.

These attacks coincided with the first mass executions of resistance people and hostages in the northern zone. At this time, too, the Gestapo uncovered a resistance group based on the personnel of the Musée de l'Homme in Paris. When one of these intellectuals, the engineer Jacques Bonsergent, was shot by the Germans, Aragon wrote a poem denouncing the execution, entitled "X . . . Français," which appeared in the Swiss review *La Suisse Contemporaine*. The Pétain government was urged by the Gestapo to arrest him, and the Vichy censors took the *N.R.F.* attack on him as a directive, "advising" *Poésie* and other French reviews not to print anything written by him.

It was time to be more careful. From then on, little of Aragon's work was published in France under his own name. His pseudonyms during the remainder of the war became numerous, but his style was easily recognizable to friends under a dozen names, such as François la Colère, Georges Meyzargues, Arnaud de Saint-Romain, or even in some tract or appeal which went unsigned.

Thus far, the arrests had not touched the embryonic

organization of the Writers' Committee, and messengers continued to arrive regularly in Nice with articles and messages from Paris. Two writers, René Laporte and Claude-André Puget, were frequent visitors at the Aragons' apartment, where Elsa Triolet had plunged into the writing of her first long novel, *Le Cheval Blanc*, and Aragon was busy completing his novel *Aurélien*, which he had begun in Carcassonne.

Already both began to tire of the dreary people who had flocked to the Riviera during the occupation, the rich French who proposed to weather out the storm in comfortable surroundings, the rich refugees from other countries who complained more of their personal troubles than of the fate of those around them, the spies, the collaborationists, the pro-Nazi royalists. Elsa Triolet has described, in an article in *Poésie*, some of these queer characters, the phantoms they met in this vortex of bitter disillusionment and confusion.

Now the German repression in Paris and the north became more intense. Towards the end of December 1941 the newspapers carried the bare news of the death and deportation of many of their friends, several of whom they had seen on their recent trip to Paris. The first to fall before the German firing squads was Gabriel Péri, foreign-affairs commentator of the Communist newspaper *Humanité,* who had been a close personal friend and colleague of Aragon, and a man of rare journalistic experience and skill. At about the same time, twenty-seven political prisoners accused of being Communists were turned over by the French to the Germans as hostages. The day after the assassination of a German colonel by unknown assailants all twenty-seven were taken from the detention camp in Châteaubriant and shot in reprisal.

Châteaubriant set a terrible precedent. It was the first publicized incident of innocent hostages being shot as an example for the acts of others. Obviously Vichy and the Germans sought to condone their action by labeling the victims as Communists, but if no protest were made mass executions would become commonplace. In the first days of 1942 a special messenger brought Aragon letters and documents containing full details on the Châteaubriant executions.

Aragon immediately wrote the most significant of his resistance appeals, the one of which he is today most proud, and which had, perhaps, the most important effect in changing the attitude of Frenchmen towards the Germans. It was entitled *Les Martyrs* and signed simply, "For the martyrs, their witness." The text was smuggled abroad and was carried on every Allied radio station beamed to France.

A short time later the Gestapo struck directly at the writers' organization. A second number of *La Libre Pensée* had appeared late in the summer of 1941. Early in 1942 the first number of *Les Lettres Françaises,* organ of the National Writers' Committee, was brought out by Jacques Decour, almost at the same time that the Gestapo rounded up the staff of the Musée de l'Homme. After diligent search they discovered that Decour and Georges Politzer had directed *La Libre Pensée,* and concluded that they were most certainly involved in the new Writers' Committee publication. Hoping, perhaps, to make these men talk, the Vichy secret police (which now had a section working in Paris to assist the Germans) arrested Decour, Politzer and Jacques Solomon. In May the French police turned them over to the Germans and the three were shot.

None of the men had given any details of the writers' organization, nor of their methods of work, but a period of pause and re-organization was essential. If the arrests and executions continued, France's leading intellectuals might be silenced, and the growing resistance movement deprived of its leadership.

* * *

In the spring of 1942, the mountebank who had

helped start *Confluences* ran off with the review's funds, leaving the bills to be paid by anyone willing to carry on. The review had a very mediocre reputation, and from a literary point of view, was a feeble effort. René Tavernier came to Nice to ask Aragon if he should take over and try to keep the review alive. Aragon advised him to do so, promising his support in an attempt to transform *Confluences* into a literary review capable of counterbalancing the influence of the *Nouvelle Revue Française,* edited by Drieu La Rochelle. The style and tone of the magazine changed quickly and *Confluences* took a leading place in French letters, a position it maintained even after the liberation.

In the spring of 1942 Aragon began two books which were printed in Switzerland in 1943, *Brocéliande* and *En Français dans le Texte.* Besides seeing writers he was in touch with the artist Henri Matisse, for whom he wrote an essay to accompany a collection of reproductions of Matisse paintings published in Paris under the title of *Thèmes et Variations.* Matisse did a series of portraits of Aragon at this time.

The Aragon home in Nice was open to many new and old friends. Seghers, Pia and Tavernier were regular visitors. Paulhan came often and finally Roger Martin du Gard came, drawn by admiration for the talent of Elsa Triolet. Tristan Tzara, a friend of many years' standing, dropped over from Sanary and was persuaded to begin writing again. In March Aragon's mother died at Cahors. After attending her funeral he visited the artists and writers in that area, including Lurçat, André Wurmser and Georges Sadoul.

The spirit and work of the writers in the south had changed completely since 1940. Vichy now acted as a stooge for the Germans, who had to resort to repressive measures to keep the French in check. It was now possible to talk openly among friends and not fear denunciation, to ask any writer to write a clandestine tract, to distribute clandestine pamphlets to people almost anywhere. The public as a whole was becoming involved in the plot to drive the Germans out. The shootings of May only confirmed this trend, although they momentarily broke contact with Paris and halted the open work of writers in the north.

In July 1942 the Aragons went back to Villeneuve and rented a house near the Seghers. That summer Villeneuve was again a center of great activity. Editors from the three resistance reviews, *Poésie, Confluences* and *Fontaine* (Jean Roire, manager of *Fontaine,* had come directly from Algiers upon his liberation from prison, where his wife and children had kept him company, met there to coördinate their activity, and to divide the manuscripts which reached them. Travelers from Paris arrived regularly.

Here they learned that the National Committee of Writers had been reconstituted, some months after Decour's death. Claude Morgan had taken over the editorship of *Les Lettres Françaises.* At the same time a number of vigorous writers had joined the National Writers' Committee in Paris, including Paul Eluard, Jean Lescure, Jean-Paul Sartre and the modest young designer Jean Bruller, who had set up the clandestine Éditions de Minuit, and whom none knew until after the liberation as the "Vercors" whose writings they all had read. Early in the autumn of 1942 the publication of *Les Lettres* was resumed.

That summer the Aragons visited Dieulefit, in the Drôme Department, with Seghers and made contact with the many writers there. While on this trip the Aragons prepared for the period of clandestinity which they knew was just ahead. They found an abandoned chalet at Comps, in the mountains above Dieulefit, where they installed two German refugee friends condemned to death by the Gestapo. It was agreed that should anything happen they themselves would go into hiding there.

After the sultry atmosphere of spy-ridden Nice, the

Aragons enjoyed the pure air of the mountains and relaxed in the free atmosphere of this independent island of French thought. Aragon had come to realize in the past months how essential it was for him to live closer to persons who thought as he did, and who were working for the liberation of the country. In Dieulefit a wall of comradeship would protect them and a discreet silent people would respect their anonymity.

Hundreds of intellectuals, writers, artists, teachers, poets, Catholics, Protestants and Jews, had already found such a refuge at Dieulefit. Without premeditation they had gravitated into this mountain area where the French Huguenots had fled in the 17th century after the revocation of the Edict of Nantes.

Dieulefit was well situated, secure amid its towering hills from too frequent visits of the police. Midway between it and the next village of Bourdeaux was the sacred grove of oak trees, where the council of Huguenot elders had met regularly centuries before to conduct the affairs of state of the independent Protestant community in France until social and religious peace was restored to the country. Now once again the leader of the French Protestant community, Pastor Boegner, had taken refuge in Dieulefit, where he met with other Protestant leaders to issue protests against the violations of the rights of man perpetrated by the German and Vichy authorities. Only 60 kilometers on inner mountain roads from Avignon and barely 100 from Lyons, this was an ideal point for maintaining contact with writers elsewhere. It was within easy reach of a score of printing presses where underground work could be done.

From Dieulefit the Aragons went to Lyons, where they held conferences with Rousseaux, Stanislas Fumet, Tavernier and many others. Back in Villeneuve, Aragon completed his last "legal" poems for *En Français dans le Texte*. On the way home they stopped off at St. Rémy de Provence to visit the blind poet, Mauron, and his wife, Marie Mauron. They returned to Nice only in October.

When the announcement of the Allied landings in North Africa came, the Aragons were ready. They packed their few belongings and prepared to terminate the period of their "legal life" under Vichy. The real struggle was about to begin.

* * *

Axis troops marched into unoccupied France on November 11, 1942. When Italian troops from Vintimiglia entered Nice the Aragons had disappeared. Gestapo and Ovra agents swarmed through the area, seeking the remnants of the Vichy "armistice army," which had vanished in large part with their arms into the mountains flanking the Rhône valley and into the foothills of the Alps. They had long lists compiled well in advance of important people they believed had been working against them under the relative protection of the Vichy regime. The resistance movement informed the Aragons that they were on those lists, and they were given every assistance in their flight.

After a short stay with friends in Villeneuve-les-Avignon, Aragon fled to the chalet near Comps, six kilometers above Dieulefit. Two weeks later Elsa rejoined him and their German friends. They remained in the hideout at Comps until the end of the year. Here Aragon edited a collection of Jacques Decour's humanistic studies of German literature and philosophy, later published clandestinely by the Editions de Minuit in Paris, as a vivid reminder that Frenchmen appreciated the true culture of Germany better than the Nazis.

During their short stay in the mountains the Aragons could gauge how thoroughly France was preparing for her liberation. All about them the first maquis units were being formed, and their village was the headquarters of one of the earliest and most active of these groups. Every day young men threatened with being conscripted for forced labor in Germany flocked into their mountain retreat to join the maquis.

The resistance movement called on Aragon to follow up his previous work among the writers in the south, to expand the clandestine press, and to write pamphlets and books with which to strengthen the morale of the Resistance. Confident now that France was recovering her old vitality, Louis and Elsa Aragon returned to Lyons on January 1, 1943, without identification papers, lodging or ration tickets, to resume their underground work. Tavernier offered them the shelter of his large Monplaisir home, where they lived for six months in the editorial offices of *Confluences*, under the mansard roof.

Hidden at *Confluences*, Aragon arranged a series of meetings with the writers in Lyons, and early in 1943 they formally founded the National Writers' Committee for the southern zone. The committee soon had local representatives in every large city and town throughout the south. It included most of the writers with whom Aragon had maintained informal contact since 1940.

In addition to the heavy load he already carried, Aragon conceived the idea of using the nucleus of the Writers' Committee to form a broad committee of the liberal professions, from which were successively developed other national committees. Within a few months committees of university professors, secondary-school teachers, doctors, artists, lawyers, magistrates and journalists had been established, had issued manifestoes, and were actively blocking collaboration with the Germans.

The central inter-professional committee was composed of the Catholic writer, Stanislas Fumet, the winner of the 1917 Prix Goncourt, Henri Malherbe, the current winner of the Grand Prix of the Académie Française, Jean Prevost (who died fighting the Germans in the battle of the Vercors the following year); an editor from *Confluences*, Auguste Angles, and Aragon.

Having organized the members of the liberal arts into the resistance movement, they soon found it necessary to coördinate the work of these intellectuals in each community, so that all the leaders in these fields could work together on local issues. For this purpose, coördinating committees of the arts and sciences, called the Etoiles, were formed in hundreds of communities in southern France. The central committee issued a regular monthly review for all the professions, bearing the same name, *Etoiles,* of which Aragon was named editor. Nineteen numbers were distributed up to the liberation, rallying the intellectuals in defense of their arrested colleagues, issuing broad directives on their work, popularizing the assistance these professional groups could give to the armed maquis forces in the hills.

By the middle of 1943 these committees were well developed throughout the whole of southern France. They flowered in 1944 and played a tremendous role in mobilizing French opinion to participate in the national uprising of June, July and August in support of the Allied invasions.

The first of these committees, which Aragon considered his greatest contribution to the resistance movement, was the National Medical Committee. He wrote the first manifesto calling for its formation, personally recruited leading doctors to become members, and presided at its first meetings. He even edited a popular, practical manual of first aid for maquis units, and another advising them how to form their field medical services.

Aragon was as proud of this thin first-aid manual as of any volume of poetry or novel he ever wrote. He guided the work of this committee always towards practical support of the guerrilla forces, as the blows of these mobile units multiplied through the autumn of 1943. He saw to it that quiet country-village practitioners in each of the areas where maquis units were operating should be on permanent emergency call to care for the wounded men. The Committee organized hidden hospitals in the mountains and staffed them with young volunteer doctors and girls trained as field nurses. It prepared lists of civilian doctors and nurses ready to move out into the clandestine military resistance units when the national uprising should come.

His role was equally important in the formation of the National Committee of Journalists, which ran the entire clandestine press of the southern zone. At the moment of liberation, members of this committee were publishing more than 200 newspapers with a circulation of well over 100,000 copies per week.

Another group which Aragon considered vital to the movement was the National Committee of Jurists and Magistrates. The many violations of Vichy decrees regarding the registration and deportation of young men to forced labor in Germany had put a great burden on the courts. Many magistrates had already shown their disdain for Vichy decrees. But now that the enemy was installed in full occupancy everywhere, it became apparent that to uphold such laws was to aid and abet the enemy.

Working quietly through the legal profession the National Committee of Jurists soon guaranteed that few patriots were brought to trial. Its members refused to hand down sentences for a variety of patriotic activities, and saw to it that men and women threatened with arrest were warned sufficiently in advance to take to the maquis. In a few short months early in 1943, the committee forced the Germans and their Vichy henchmen to pass outside legal French channels and to conduct their operations in true bandit fashion, with secret raids, secret arrests, secret confinements and summary court proceedings.

In the same spring of 1943 three publishing houses were established in the south by the Writers' Committee, the Bibliothèque Française, the Editions des Franc-Tireurs et Partisans, and the Editions des Femmes Françaises, which were to issue popular editions of resistance literature in a dozen scattered cities. One of the first books published in this series was Aragon's protest against the execution of writers and professional people by the Germans, *Le Crime Contre l'Esprit*. It was later reprinted by the Editions de Minuit in Paris.

The National Writers' Committee in Lyons maintained regular contact with the Writers' Committee in Paris. This was now preparing to issue some of the outstanding works of the clandestine period in book form through the Editions de Minuit, which up to then had produced everything in mimeograph sheets. After the occupation of the south Pierre Seghers was assigned to make frequent trips to Paris for this purpose.

The Paris committee agreed that conditions were still too precarious for the original division of the National Writers' Committee into two zones to be changed. They decided, however, to maintain a more centralized organization for the publication of anti-German literature in each of the two zones, and to collaborate more closely with Jean Bruller (Vercors) and Yvonne Desvignes in furnishing texts for publication in his clandestine Editions de Minuit. Paul Eluard represented the committee in the new book enterprise.

Louis Aragon, while taking no part in production, played an important role in this work. Two of the Editions de Minuit books were written by him and he supplied introductions for three more. As head of the Writers' Committee of the southern zone, he was responsible also for assigning subjects or for helping edit six more books in the series.

* * *

In July 1943, when all this work was well under way, the resistance movement decided that Aragon was too well-known a figure to be safe in a large city like Lyons. They promised to find him a place where he could escape observation. The Aragons wanted to return to Dieulefit, but this was rejected as dangerous because too many people there knew him personally. Shortly thereafter he and Elsa moved to a small house in the village of St. Donat, where we found them. From there, they could readily reach Lyons for the regular monthly meetings. They were almost the only strangers in the place, and were known to the villagers under false names.

Every precaution was taken in handling material for publication. If a pamphlet was needed, some emissary would visit the writer assigned to the job and set the deadline. On the date set the writer put his manuscript in the designated place, often a rural post box, or a hollow tree, or a hole among the rocks. He never saw the third person who picked up this single manuscript (copies could not be kept by the author) and passed it on to an editor and then to a printer. Months might pass before the writer saw it in print.

Meetings took place in quiet suburban streets, where two friends coming from opposite directions would accidentally meet and have a friendly chat. Between meetings, Aragon directed this work. His travelling representative was the secretary of the Writers' Committee, Georges Sadoul, who bore a charmed life as he travelled the length and breadth of southern France, his briefcase crammed with manuscripts or printed tracts and booklets.

In their little cottage at St. Donat, where the local inhabitants thought Louis and Elsa were *miliciens* (pro-German police agents) because of their many trips away from the village, they both continued to write, despite their manifold duties. Here Aragon wrote the powerful ode which pilloried the Germans and their French collaborators, *Le Musée Grévin*. To this period also belong some of his most moving short lyrics, such as "Celui qui Chante dans les Supplices," "Absents de Paris," "Prélude à la Diane Française," a number of outstanding short stories such as "Les Bons Voisins" and "Le Pénitent 43," and a host of articles, pamphlets, broadsheets and polemic articles for the clandestine reviews and newspapers.

Elsa Triolet was no less active. Because of her Russian

origin, she was often called away on special missions. Russian prisoners sent into wild parts of the country as garrison troops frequently fled to the mountains. Elsa would induce them to furnish valuable information and join the maquis. Despite these many trips Elsa completed one of the best short novels of the resistance movement, *Les Amants d'Avignon*.

An indication of the speed with which manuscripts could now be moved across the country and put into print was the publication of a book by each of the Aragons. In August and September 1943 Louis wrote *Le Musée Grévin*, while Elsa put the finishing touches to *Les Amants d'Avignon*. Both were published in Paris less than a month later, in October, by the Editions de Minuit.

* * *

In the early autumn of 1943 the National Writers' Committee decided to call one more over-all clandestine meeting in Paris, to settle the details of their final phase of work before the national uprising. For this the Aragons made their second trip to Paris, with completely forged documents this time. As a publication schedule was to be set up at this meeting they carried the manuscripts of several books with them. The manuscripts were in Elsa's ample handbag, with *La Façon de Vivre et de Mourir de Gabriel Péri* right on top. The trip seemed at first to be going off well. There was no longer the danger of the heavily guarded demarcation line they had faced in 1941. But suddenly at one station Gestapo agents came on board and began a thorough search of the whole train. The Aragons gave everything up for lost.

A soldier in field-green stepped into their compartment and began a minute inspection of all documents and all luggage. There were several women in the crowded compartment, and their handbags were searched before Elsa's turn came. Her handbag had a shiny new zipper on it. The soldier picked up the bag and put his fingers on the handle of the zipper.

"We knew we were finished," Aragon told me, describing the scene. "And then an officer in the corridor called the soldier. He handed the bag back to Elsa and went out. When he came back he had forgotten that there was one more handbag to search. He looked in and then moved on. We didn't dare breathe."

At the station in Paris, Paul Eluard and his wife were waiting for them. It was one of the dramatic moments of the war for Aragon. Neither of the men had spoken to each other since Aragon's violent break with the surrealists in 1931. Many years and many tragic events had put them on the same road together again.

This brief visit was otherwise uneventful. The manuscripts were delivered, and the Aragons reported on their work in the south at a Committee meeting which Paul Eluard, Claude Morgan, Jean Paulhan, Jean Bruller, Jean Lescure, Pierre de Lescure, Jean-Paul Sartre and a few others attended. Plans for helping the Committee of National Liberation prepare the *soulèvement nationale* were elaborated.

The conference was a timely one. The various resistance movements had grown in strength and had achieved unity as a result of the latest events. The endless arguments about the possible pro-Allied role of Vichy had been terminated by the German occupation of Vichy territory. The proximity of Allied troops, the major defeats of Axis forces at Stalingrad, Libya, Tunis, and now in Italy, and the promise of an early landing in France itself had galvanized the entire nation and settled all minor differences among the writers, as it had among the people at large. Before the end of October the Aragons went back to work at their home in St. Donat.

* * *

Aragon was very strict with himself and with his colleagues. He was profoundly convinced that their work was no less useful than bearing arms, and that in the strange war of resistance it was one of the most vital phases of combat. He never doubted his ability, the ability of the resistance writers as a whole, to incite masses of people to open struggle against the enemy. The formation of an aroused people into efficient fighting units or resistance groups was a task for other patriots, assigned to that particular job. He insisted that none of his writers should participate in such work.

I remember his anger when Jean Marcenac, a talented young poet and liaison man for the Writers' Committee, returned after "wasting" two months fighting with the maquis forces. He had been sent on an important mission carrying manuscripts to a distant city two months before, but on his way back he had been caught up in the fever of revolt and joined a group of friends in the maquis. In my presence Aragon gave him a tongue lashing for leaving his post of duty.

When Marcenac had gone Aragon told me of his escape from a German prison camp in 1943. "He's one of our most promising young poets. I understand why he did it. How could we expect young men who have been through what he has not to hate the Germans? The chance to fight them again must have been irresistible." He might complain about the over-active role of some members of his group, but he himself often had a natural urge to participate in the fighting phase of resistance, to experience its emotions and dangers.

Once, in July 1944, he and Elsa were invited to be present when arms were dropped by parachute in the region of St. Donat. If they did not appear they would have been suspected as traitors. So one night they climbed to a plateau high above their village, watching tensely under the brilliant stars until the planes came and dropped their precious load. Once the arms and equipment had been hidden in a nearby cave, the group scattered. The Aragons returned to their village at dawn. They had hardly slept an hour when they were aroused by German fighter planes overhead, machine-gunning the streets of St. Donat. Messengers reported that German flying columns of tanks and trucks were racing on the village from several directions. Louis and Elsa had just time to throw on their clothes again and to escape to the nearby vineyards on the slopes above the village, hugging the shadows to escape the bullets of strafing German planes. All day long the Germans plundered and ravaged the homes and people of St. Donat.

The troops who participated in these punitive expeditions during this period of national uprising were not courageous. They always retired to some fortified garrison town in the valleys at nightfall. When the Aragons returned from the hills to help their neighbors clean up the devastation, they found their house pillaged, its doors smashed in. Fifty-seven girls and women, from 13 to 58 years of age, had been raped; eight men killed. Every shop and house had been sacked. The simplest household treasures of the small community had been carried off by these modern vandals. Without loss of time Aragon published a number of clandestine tracts in answer to the Vichy propaganda of that day, which blamed such depredations on the maquis forces, who by their illegal activities brought German retribution on the innocent. Aragon explained that these punitive expeditions were the last acts of the trapped and desperate Nazis, hoping to paralyze the people by fear; and that the only answer to such acts of sadism was open revolt.

In those last months the Aragons were provided with a car. They visited the Drôme area maquis headquarters regularly to sit in on councils of war, to give their advice on the state of public opinion, and to assist the maquis command in its appeals for support from the population. When the electrifying news of the Normandy landing reached them, they immediately disobeyed another of their rules and began editing the combat newspaper for their area, *La Drôme en Armes*. From its first issue it had a circulation of 20,000 copies, supplementing equally large distribution of two other papers published at Dieulefit in the southern part of the department, to which they also contributed regularly, *La Résistance de la Drôme* and *Le Patriote de la Drôme*. These papers are vivid and alive even today, with their accounts of the local engagements which marked the national uprising and made a swiftly moving battlefield of this entire area. They contain perhaps the best account published of the vast battle of the Vercors plateau which tied up four precious German divisions in the mountains of France in the weeks between the Normandy invasion and the southern Riviera invasion.

* * *

When the mobile French and American tank columns had liberated Lyons and swept on up the Saône and Ain Rivers towards Alsace, the Aragons closed their little home in St. Donat, said farewell to the people among whom they had lived such stirring moments of history, and who now for the first time learned their true identity, and returned to Lyons. Here Aragon was busy for several weeks inquiring into the fate of various colleagues, organizing the first public meetings of the Writers' Committee, and supervising the work of the new official Ministry of Information offices for the area.

After five years of such intensive work everything inside him cried out for freedom to write, to avoid being chained to some routine job in the machinery of state that now must be built from the ruins. He had been proposed, prior to the liberation, as Commissioner of the Republic for the Marseilles area. He found a replacement. Then he was urged to take the same assignment at Toulouse. Happily there was his good friend Jean Cassou, a native of Toulouse, whom he could recommend as much more qualified than himself. Temporarily, he was free, and he rushed to complete his book of poetry, *La Diane Française*, and to prepare the outline of a novel on the resistance period.

But he could not escape so easily. With the liberation of Paris, *Ce Soir,* the afternoon newspaper of which he had been co-editor before the war, was revived. Jean-Richard Bloch, his former colleague, was still abroad, having fled from imminent arrest in 1941. Aragon was needed to carry on until Bloch's return. When he reached Paris he could not refuse. Not until Bloch came back in December was he free at last.

His interest in the Writers' Committee remained as keen as before. He found time to plan with Jean Bruller, Pierre de Lescure, and Paul Eluard, the republication of all the literary works which the Writers' Committee had issued during the occupation. He helped establish *Les Lettres Françaises* as the living successor of the pre-war *Nouvelle Revue Française,* and he helped bring those two reviews of the south which had been so valuable in the struggle, *Poésie* and *Confluences,* back to Paris. Early in November he managed to get away to attend the first congress of the now free National Writers' Committee in Toulouse. There he saw Cassou, who had been gravely wounded in the last days of liberation, and some of his other missing colleagues. But in checking with one another, the writers learned of many others who had died while fighting in the maquis or had been deported to Germany.

The story of Louis Aragon during the German occupation of France is in fact the story of the resistance movement through the experiences of one man. It is the story, moreover, of a very conscious leader of the resistance movement, a man who was instrumental in organizing the work of dozens of writers against the conquerors, a man who denounced the enemy to his people and aroused in them a new sense of confidence in themselves and in their power to help free their own land.

Louis Aragon himself would not claim to have been the leading writer, or organizer of writers, in this period. He would attribute the success of their work to many lesser-known figures. But it is the miracle of France that it produced at least five men as active as he was, as powerful in their writing: Paul Eluard, Jean Bruller, Jacques Decour, Pierre Seghers, and Jean Lescure, besides a host of others who fought no less bravely. Parts of Aragon's story bear the stamp of heroism, yet he would be the first to deny that he played a hero's part.

He regarded what he did as the duty of a new type of soldier in a new type of warfare. Since the liberation called for a struggle of the whole people, he felt that the writers had accomplished their tasks more effectively than the soldiers had done theirs during the fighting in 1940. The return of confidence, the certainty in his own power and strength, which shows in the actions and writing of Aragon as the tide of resistance rose to expel the conquerors, are typical of the rebirth of France and of the French people. Aragon never allowed himself to be cut off, as were so many older French writers, from the flood-tide of youthful resistance in France. He was a vital part of it, as he is of the new France today.

PETER C. RHODES

ARAGON BETWEEN WARS

As I LOOK back on the young man I knew in that sinister world between wars, whose portents of hellfire the foolish mistook for the dawn, I realize that the proud role Louis Aragon has played in the years of the German occupation and since, as folk poet and folk hero, was already forecast in his earliest manifestation. The first time I saw Aragon was in the beginning nineteen-twenties (he was not three years older than the century). He came to see me in my room in an old hotel of the rue de l'Université which James Joyce had recommended to me. He sat in a musty red-plush chair, his back to the balcony that looked north over the left bank to the Seine. In the shadow, his tense, prehensile, handsome face was a dark flame. I knew he had fought as a simple soldier in the War. I said to him:

"I suppose you're glad at least the War is over."

"Is it?" he replied bitterly. "If you call this 'peace,' what makes you say it is preferable to the trenches?"

In those days, Aragon loved André Gide, whose lucid prose contains the kind of ambiguity into which young men of spirit can read anything they want to. *Les Caves du Vatican* was Aragon's predilection, the *acte gratuit*, the *crime sans motif*, of Lafcadio. By temperament, he was an anarchist, a revolutionary romantic. But even in those days, when he followed the Dada of Tristan Tzara and set off *surréalisme* with sensational literary explosions, it was evident that Aragon belonged to the organism of French culture. Tradition was visible in his fine, hard prose which expressed revolt from bourgeois

Europe, from a "peace" that was masked war. An organic culture was evident in the young man's poise and cool intelligence, which kept his emotional power, his *willed* excesses, in place. The paradox of this "enemy of the past" had its source in France's strongest literary and intellectual roots, even as the art of Cézanne was—as he knew—rooted in the museums.

I believe it was this year, or possibly the next, that the adolescent son of Léon Daudet, the virulent reactionary pamphleteer who edited *l'Action Française* with Charles Maurras, made the perfect gesture of youth's disgust with "that peace" by committing suicide in a taxi. Young Daudet was one of a group of literary anarchists, and Aragon took me to see them. Paris, at the time, was full of violent infant prodigies, designing death for the Louvre and the French language. And Aragon among them was as visibly distinct as a line in a Raphael drawing from a blur; he spoke their phrases, but clearly, so that they were transfigured. The reason for the difference was obvious: instinctively, the man had discipline, and was being nourished from his roots.

In 1923 I happened to be with him the night we learned of the death of Maurice Barrès. Barrès, as a chauvinist nationalist *deputé,* stood of course on the other side of the barricades. But Aragon spoke of him with respect, as a great literary figure. The *culte du moi* of the early Barrès novels had become a *culte du pays.* To Aragon, an impulse of egoism, acceptable to his romantic anarchism, had miscarried, which was no reason for not doing it justice. He wanted to send an obituary at once to some paper, and he came up to my room, late that evening, to write it. I watched him at work at my table. He sat there with a Blake-like grace; and his words came lucidly. He wrote fairly. The dissociation of ideas, which Rémy de Gourmont had characterized as the trait of good thinking and good writing, was natural for Louis Aragon.

His sympathy (daring, in a Dadaist) for what was

sound in Barrès was prophetic. The soil, that the nationalist loved and wrongly served, was part of Aragon's more organic vision. Differently, not alone from Barrès and Gide, but also from his associates of that time, Breton, Soupault, et al., Aragon's romantic egoism was to adumbrate into an active sense of his epoch, of France, and of the world. The *self* which Aragon discovered was organic, lacking no social, no spiritual dimensions. One felt this, already, in his early prose; one felt it in his readiness to fuse literature with action. Later, one felt it in his communism. And the world found it, full-flowering, at last, in his lyrics of the Fall in which the most intimate personal tenderness and national bereavement are fused without artifice.

My memory of our many meetings leaps to the last time I saw Aragon: the year before the second War. We knew it was coming; coming fast. We knew it was already being fought in Spain, with the phony democracies hypocritically aiding the Fascists who, in Germany and Italy, at least were honest in their hatred of Spain's Republic. We knew, also, that it was being surreptitiously fought by the Chamberlains and the City of London and the French conservatives against Russia. In my recollection of those last talks, the five last years before the Deluge are dramatically essenced. I was in Paris, before and after my last visits to Spain. I saw Romain Rolland in Vézelay (his old, beloved hands playing the last *Bagatelles* of Beethoven on the piano); I stayed with Gide on the rue Vaneau; I visited Jacques Maritain in his humble suburban home near Paris. There was something sacramental about these last communions; an End was near, and we knew it. And what was Aragon doing? With Jean-Richard Bloch, my friend whom the police of Paris secretly saved from the Gestapo, Aragon was editing the evening paper, *Ce Soir*. The years had solidified his fire. The lyrical in him, always clear because its roots were organic, had now become the man, at home in France, at home in Russia, in Europe, in the world.

I had seen the start of this final phase of Aragon's evolution in 1935, at the time of the Congress of Writers held in Paris for the Defense of Culture. I spent a good part of my first day, after my arrival and before the congress opened, walking the boulevards with Aragon. And he explained to me the abortive counter-revolution of the previous year (the *Affaire Stavisky*), the rottenness of the huge middle classes of Paris. The congress, he said, was part of the strategy of counter-attack. If the democratic forces were mobilized in time, the enemy might not strike. There were hopeful men at that congress; some of the Communist leaders were most hopeful. But Aragon knew already what was coming. The future was red with blood. His mood was acceptance. And it energized him. In his earliest *surréaliste* days, he had been nourished, almost unaware, by the soil and tradition of France. Now, a faithful and disciplined member of a party which despised religion, he moved with that freedom within the acceptance of necessity which—whatever he might name it—is religious. The one solid front in all the western world was the front of the Fascists! Our scattered forces were already under fire. This was the time to march forward. The later Aragon of the National Writers' Committee, under the heel of the Gestapo, was already limned in 1935.

And now, at our latest meeting in 1938, he was already the soldier. He spoke to me lucidly of Russia, calmly commenting on my criticisms of the wisdom of the Stalinists in dealing with Trotsky. I did not agree with all he said; I did not know enough of Russia, which I had not visited since 1931, either to agree or dissent. But I felt the tragic sobriety behind the poet's words and the poet's actions. He was already in an enemy-occupied France, an enemy-occupied Europe. He knew it.

The poet, I have often said, is the *exact* reporter of the real. He is the one precisionist. (His data go far beyond the limited domain of science.) In this sense, Aragon was and is a poet.

The man since the beginning of his career has worked from an integral ethic—the same, in very different terms, can be said of Malraux—whose source is a profound and complete connection with the whole. It comes to him, not metaphysically or abstractly, but in terms of France, of contemporary problems, in terms of men and women. His aesthetic, as a significant creator of French letters, is a unitary *ethic* which informs his personal no less than his public life. Péguy would call it Aragon's *mystique*. Within this kind of *pre-rational* soil, good works and good poetry can flower.

WALDO FRANK

SAINT-POL ROUX, OR HOPE

*This is the first article by Aragon to be published after the
defeat of France. He wrote it in a white heat, shortly after
he was demobilized in July 1940, on learning the circumstances of the aged poet's death. Saint-Pol Roux was living
in what he called the Manor of Coecilian, in the village of
Camaret, not far from Brest, with his daughter Divine and
a single servant, Marie, when the Germans overran Brittany.
A few days after the occupation of Camaret, four drunken
soldiers broke into his grounds and attacked his daughter.
Her screams brought the servant and the old man running
to her assistance. The soldiers shot Marie and beat the
poet off with their rifle butts. Saint-Pol Roux died a few days
later.*

*The article was published under Aragon's name in the
autumn, 1940, number of* Poésie. *Since* Poésie *was published legally, Aragon had to put over his point by indirec-
tion, but the Vichy censorship cut several paragraphs besides
which might have displeased the conquerors. In the first
issue of* Poésie *published after the liberation the editors reprinted the article in its entirety, and it is this version which
is given here.*

ON NOVEMBER 11, 1918, as bells rang out the armistice
of the First World War, poetry lost Guillaume Apollinaire, the starry-headed singer. The Spanish War, which
opened with the death of Federico Garcia Lorca, ended
in the last spring of *our* peace, just as Antonio Machado,
inventor of the machine for making poems, died on the
very threshold of France. Our own disaster likewise

draws to a close with the assassination of a poet. In mangled France, as we counted our dead, we recognized among them Saint-Pol Roux, known as the Magnificent, whose destiny was so strange that his very death is enveloped in the mystery of the forbidden and one hesitates to tell how he perished there at the tip of Brittany where phantoms meet the sea. Even while he lived his voice had been stilled.

The day will come when our young people will wonder why we allowed him to be so neglected during his lifetime. We are as yet far from acknowledging the part played by the author of *Anciennetés* in remolding French verse, in leading it away from its queer metrics and its cursed images. No one shines more than he by his absence from the textbooks of the Lanson, Doumic type. A black diamond. However, had I one of his books at hand, particularly *Le Bouc Emissaire* [*The Scapegoat*] I would enjoy demonstrating how the 7-5 or 5-7 cadence of the alexandrine, which was to reach glorious heights during the days of Apollinaire, was born. But Saint-Pol Roux was not torn from us by death alone. His death is linked with the invasion, and contains symbols which will be unraveled at a later time. I only want to relate under what circumstances the fate of the Magnificent became known to me.

It was the first of June, at Dunkirk. Hell was raining from the sky, and we had passed beyond the ruined city. We had seen the wretched steamer that was to have saved us sail away at dawn, loaded with Moroccans, leaving us on the narrow jetty without much hope that another boat would come. We could feel the sand of Malo-les-bains in our pockets and defeat in our hearts. My boys, those thirty students, whom I had taught the mocking gestures of obedience and the elements of first aid, exhausted by their trek to the coast under the constant fire of the enemy from two sides, squatted on the cobblestones facing the sea, where ten foundered vessels reminded us of our probable fate. It was then that they began to sing "Les Filles de Camaret": *

> *The curtains of our bed*
> *Are made in cloth of red. . . .*

And suddenly the song with all its blasphemies carried me far away to a place I never expected to see again, to that blue bay with its blood-red rocks, where as in a dream I saw the lord of the manor of Coecilian, Saint-Pol Roux the Magnificent. At that jumping-off place, while France seemed to be going through her death agony in the sea before us, this thought might well have been my last.

I did not know, I did not understand at that moment, how strange it was to be dreaming of that particular poet, to whom, about fifteen years earlier, during the most turbulent period of my youth, my friends and I had tendered as a crown of thorns the homage which a deaf world refused.

(I can still see that sunny afternoon at the Closerie des Lilas when we acclaimed Saint-Pol Roux at a banquet. What is left of it all? Regardless of the pretences and the errors, the fact remains that the forgotten Saint-Pol Roux once found a fanatical welcome among those for whom poetry meant more than wisdom, among those who wanted to erect a monument to his integrity and his dissent. Perhaps the return of the Magnificent to Paris roused up for a moment the indifferent city, which has always been more easily captivated by a pretty hat than by a poetic image. Perhaps his return avenged a little the unheralded and unnoticed return of the dying Rimbaud to Marseilles. Thanks to that strange evening, celebrated like an eclipse or the passage of a comet, when Saint-Pol Roux died at last his name was more than a word en-

* "The Girls of Camaret," a bawdy song, popular in the army. Camaret was the name of the village in Brittany where Saint-Pol Roux lived and died.

graved on a tombstone to the French. For France to appreciate the work of this poet will still require many years and many upheavals. Charles Péguy himself has only recently been discovered.)

Once again on the road of defeat a vision of the lord of the manor of Coecilian recurred to me. After we had crossed and recrossed the Channel, we were moving south from Normandy in a long convoy, our vehicles full of wounded, when amid the signs of devastation, the refugees from Paris first crossed our path. Women trundling baby-carriages piled high with valises and household articles, stopped and pointed to the highway we were abandoning to the advancing enemy, calling to me, "Is this the right road to Brest? We want to go to Camaret." I called back that they were mad, that the road to the sea was open to the motorized battalions of the enemy, who were overrunning the entire countryside of Aube and the forest of Conche, as well as this road to Laigle. I shouted to them to make for the river Loire and to give up going to Brittany and Camaret. . . . It was then I heard myself speak once more the name of that town, which for me represented the Magnificent. Like Peter on the road to Calvary, I knew we were really denying our neglected poet again, abandoning him on the last reef of our country, like the symbol of our greatness and our misery trapped between the tide of steel and the spray of the sea.

We traveled then across the peaceful countryside, through fields which had not heard the tread of soldiers' feet since the days of the religious wars, through meadows where only the sound of voices singing rounds had overlapped the centuries. Step by step we had defended and left so many castles and towns, so many vibrant places where the memories of history and the tears of legends besought us not to go on without them, that at last we stopped in a region of high towers where the ghosts of Cyrano, D'Artagnan, and Captain Fracasse came to meet us. In the evenings, beside our radios, we talked of all that had been wrested from us, and here in his very own country we said with Agrippa d'Aubigné: *

The towns of the interior are the frontier towns. . . .

Our hearts and throats were filled with grief, little as we knew then for whom or for what greatness we mourned.

And when the waters had gone down from off the earth, I found myself one day in a city of ruined cloth merchants which lay in the shadow of an old town made of papier-mâché and dreams. In the streets men passed like myself, dressed in old clothes or uniforms stripped of insignia, men idle and defeated. In the Place aux Herbes was a pink fountain with a Latin inscription and a market, and the wine-growers swarmed about with their samples of wine in phials. And through the crowd went a tall man followed by a Great Dane, too noble a beast for ordinary fodder. From a poet who lived nearby, blinded and bed-ridden since the last war, but constantly recreating the world denied to his eyes, I learned that this man was Lorédan, the son of Saint-Pol Roux. At about the same time a letter from Morocco and a traveler from Paris acquainted me with the details of the terrible death of the Magnificent, and the tragedy of his daughter, named Divine in defiance of Heaven, who had been wounded and violated by fiends from Hell. Two perfunctory lines in a newspaper. The secret sores of my country are the deepest: those that are denied or passed over in silence. Today we can only honor her martyrs in our hearts, but some day we shall kiss the footprints of her nameless heroes. Who will draw up the balance sheet of the sufferings of France, the exact, the stupendous account of her real wounds, her unmentionable sacrifices, her courage so long unrecognized? I have seen men smile who had lived through indescribable horror. Only *now* do we know how to recognize beauty. . . .

* A Huguenot soldier and poet of the sixteenth century.

In this city, at the home of my friend, the poet cruci-fied in the dark, I found a large bound manuscript, a collection of poems and articles. It was the work of Saint-Pol Roux, written in his inimitable stenographic hand-writing. Chance may have brought this volume into my hands, but it contained too many sentences expressly applicable to this moment of our lives for the particular choice of material to have been accidental. The manu-script began with a poem from *Les Reposoirs de la Pro-cession* [*Stations of the Cross*], a poem called "The Cemetery with Wings," which reads:

They are gone, the little shepherd boys with the brown mustaches, from the pleasant village where the godchildren are pale as moonlight and the grandsires are the color of the stones of Calvary.

Gone to the sound of a drunkard beating a dead ass, gone to the frontier, the little ones.

The mother of their mother having passed by, crying:

"At the edge of the waters which separate our countries, I saw the barbarous plumes of the great drinkers of beer with the blond mustaches, O my pretty ones! A little of your death would save my life."

And they had answered:

"Here I am, my country!"

So spoke each little cider-drinker with the brown mus-tache from the pleasant hamlet where the godchildren are pale as moonlight and the grandsires are the color of the stones of Calvary.

Surely he was addressing us in this poem, a poem we cannot read without a shudder, a poem whose final massacre leaves us with an ironically bitter taste:

At least this tremendous barricade of corpses was to guard forever the land of the dark-haired people from the blond invaders. . . .

On rereading this manuscript, I find it is not the poetry alone which moves me. Saint-Pol Roux speaks to

me in words like life itself, so much so that I hesitate
to lift them out of their context, and confine myself to
quoting these two sentences from an answer he made to
Max Nordau after Nordau had denounced everything
that had contributed to the spiritual greatness of his period, Verlaine and Baudelaire included, as a sign of
decadence and hysteria:

"Does he not go too far in assuming that France was
disabled by her revolutionary crises, her Napoleonic
wars, and the recent blood-letting of 1870? These catas-
trophes, particularly the last one, served rather to correct
our Latin frivolity, by forcing us to recognize the brain
of the Faust who had come to place his heel upon our
breast."

I read this just as the newspapers were seriously rais-
ing the question whether the France of the spirit was
not dead, and whether this France should not be forced
to her knees like a criminal. So, all along the Calvary of
my country, I found at each "Station of the Cross" Saint-
Pol Roux the Magnificent. His voice, his life, his death
are an illustrious example to us, along with the harrowing hope he leaves us, the hope we find in his mangled
heart. To finish this article, whose only purpose is to
assure Saint-Pol Roux of a future in which he will not
be forgotten, to associate him forever with the rose without a thorn that is our France and our secret, let Saint-
Pol Roux himself speak and tell again of the village at
land's end, whither the fugitives on the road to Laigle
were going in June, and which the blond invaders would
reach before them:

ROSCANVEL

Penny picture, color of a hornpipe, village, tiny village,
where the bells seem to tinkle on the neck of an immense
stone goat, Roscanvel dips its bare feet into the shallow sea,
whose blue flesh is visible beneath the shivering sails.

O my simple destiny beneath the shade of fig trees, elms,

and yews where the piping cries of school children mingle with the songs of birds. . . .

At evening see the cormorants in mourning returning to their nests far below on the reefs of Camaret, gone since dawn, some in triangular flight, others in squadrons skimming the sea, a low flight like the long ears of a hunting dog whose body worn by the ocean would only be the remains of a carcass.

Here men laugh and weep, here they live and die as in a legend, men of earth and men of the sea. And it is always a weekday, since they toil without ceasing, and it is always Sunday because the drunkards— O the tragic faces of Brittany with their tiny periwinkle eyes—come and go continually across the fields and the moors and the thickets to the Calvaries gnawed by the ulcer of time.

I have quoted this poem from *La Rose et des Epines du Chemin* ["The Rose and Thorns of the Road"] not because it was the last in this morocco-bound manuscript which the poet Joë Bousquet had given me in Carcassonne, but because the final verse begins with a line which sums up a father's love and a martyr's destiny:

It is here, Divine, here that you were born . . .

Men of these tragic days, my countrymen, repeat softly the lesson of the Magnificent, no longer obscure to anyone:

It is here, Divine, here that you were born . . .

Here at the farthest point of the land and of thought, at the borders of France and the sea, at the frontiers of all poetry, at the limits of our hope.

Translated by Helen Burlin

THE GOOD NEIGHBORS

This lively popular story was turned out by the thousand in pamphlet form by the underground press, printed on coarse gray paper and small enough to be slipped unnoticeably even into a workman's shirt-pocket. In his younger days Aragon had written short stories full of the most daring innovations in style and method; in this he shows himself a master of the conventional forms as well. The pseudonym here used was Arnaud de Saint-Romain.

IT WAS just like in the movies. They all came pushing in together. Except that there's no revolving door in our house and eight guys crammed in our third floor walkup makes it pretty close. Especially in the summer time.

We were just about to sit down to eat. We eat supper early to save electricity. Pauline called out from the kitchen for me to put them out. She said everything would get cold. They got a big laugh out of that. Pauline came in with the soup and she was so surprised, she nearly dropped it. Our place isn't very big or fancy but it's ours. You get attached to things you've had for a long time. We have more memories than furniture, if you know what I mean.

Eight of them. The fat one was the boss. He tipped his big hat backwards and scratched his head. There was a very skinny one with big hands, like lobster claws stretching out to grab anything in sight. The others . . . well, they were like the pictures in the paper.

In two shakes, everything was topsy-turvy. I tried to reason with the fat guy. I kicked because I remembered they were supposed to have an order, a paper of some kind. That tickled them, too. It seems that nowadays it's not done that way.

The first thing Pauline got excited about was her bed-spread. They tore it off the bed in one swipe, and twisted the sheets up like a dirty handkerchief.

One guy was rummaging in the cupboard, another in the linen closet. Papers were flying around. A box full of pins was upset on the floor. They looked under the chairs and stuck long needles into the upholstery. Two or three of them just stood there, cluttering up the place.

And the language they used! When the skinny one called Pauline "Old woman," I let go. "Look here, you," I said to him. That started them off again. Everything struck them as hilarious.

The man who was searching me shook out my wallet. A lot of useless little pieces of paper I'd been too lazy to throw away fell out. My soap ration card too. He asked me all kinds of questions and insisted that my key-ring was used for goodness knows what. The fat one had got hold of the letter-holder trimmed with seashells we brought back from Tréport, and he was going over the gas bills as well as Alfred's letters. Then he wanted to know all about the people in the photos.

In the picture we took at Meudon three years before the war, I couldn't remember the guy standing behind cousin Maurice. A big fellow with a birthmark on his cheek. A friend of the Picherelles, I think. But that's all I knew. The fat guy thought that was suspicious and he started plaguing Pauline about it, so we'd trip each other up. As usual, Pauline contradicted me: "A friend of the Picherelles? Where on earth did you get such an idea? He's Madame Janneau's boyfriend. You know Madame Janneau, the corsetière."

Then I was foolish enough to say that Madame Janneau's friend was a blond and that this one was dark. And when you start arguing about the color of a person's hair. . . . The fat guy was very interested.

"There, now," he said, "why don't you two get together on these things?"

That really got my goat. What business was it of his whether the man was Madame Janneau's friend or not?

"Don't you worry," he said. "It's my business all right." And he kept fiddling with his hat.

The men who were cluttering up the room doing nothing stood there like ninepins. And was it hot!

Finally, I said to him, "When a person goes into a home he usually takes his hat off. Isn't it enough for you to tear the place apart?"

Pauline set up a howl. They were pulling her clean pillow cases out. They'd have to be washed, what with their dirty paws. . . .

The skinny one had a nasty look in his eye. "Watch out, you fat tub," he jeered at her.

"None of that stuff!" I was hopping mad but he paid no attention to me.

One of them, a short stocky man with a red mustache, looked like a plug-ugly. He was giving the sewing machine a going-over, not missing a thing. He opened the drawer, spread the contents on the floor, emptied the shuttles, unwound the thread and all the spools of silk. With a kind of feverish curiosity, he examined every piece of metal, the thingamajig for making pleats, all the gadgets Pauline considers her prize possessions. Then he'd fling them all over his shoulder. The stuff landed anywhere and an argument started when one of his pals got hit in the neck.

I said, "Gentlemen, please . . ."

This time, they didn't laugh. They both turned on me and started asking me questions about the government.

I couldn't answer them because Pauline was yelling so loud. She was struggling with a big guy and trying to snatch our wedding picture away from him. The one in the silver frame. And then when the little spoons crashed out of the cupboard drawer, I couldn't get a word in edgewise.

Finally, I showed them Marshal Pétain's picture in the place of honor on the mantelpiece. It's the one where he's stroking a dog (the family portrait, Alfred used to say). But that didn't impress them a bit.

The fat one sneered and said gruffly, "Oh, sure, that's easy, my fine friend. All you customers have a picture hung up."

The others nodded. You could see they'd been through this before.

"But what are we accused of?" asked Pauline, sniffling.

The fat one gave her a look to send shivers down your spine.

"You're not being accused of anything, Madame," he said. "You're under suspicion and that's much worse."

It's worse, all right. The skinny guy was feeling the embroidered cushion my sister-in-law Michaud made when she became blind. Suddenly he let out a whoop.

"What did I tell you?" he said. I don't know what he told anybody, but I do know that he started pulling off the petitpoint embroidery and tearing the feathers out of the pillow. Afterwards, he claimed he'd felt something hard inside. Maybe he felt it, but he didn't find it.

Pauline was screaming her head off. The skinny guy had the nerve to put his lobster claw over her mouth. And did I catch it when I tried to interfere! After all, I'm sixty-two years old. I know how to behave and I respect the laws of my country. But when they start getting rough with the ladies . . .

"Don't get yourself into a sweat," the redhead said. Actually, the place was stifling.

Two of the cops had sat down at the table and were lapping up the soup. They poured themselves some wine and clinked their glasses. When I said something about it to the fat guy, he said, "Don't try to change the subject."

I couldn't have if I'd tried. I didn't know what the subject was. I kept trying to figure out why they had come. It was probably an anonymous letter . . . people are so mean nowadays. . . . But what could the letter possibly have said?

Pauline started to sit down on the hassock. That made the skinny one suspicious. He pushed her off, tore off the fringe, and poked his hand in. She tried to open a window but they wouldn't let her, in spite of the heat. I guess they thought she might try to rouse the neighbors.

"Now, gentlemen," I said, "will you kindly tell me to what we owe the pleasure . . ."

"The pleasure! Did you say the pleasure? Are you trying to make monkeys out of us?"

I must admit I was putting it on a bit thick. The visit of these gentlemen was not exactly what you'd call a pleasure. But . . .

"But what?" asked the fat guy, sitting down in my favorite red and brown armchair, as though the whole business had worn him out. "You're beginning to get on my nerves with your phony remarks, your 'ifs' and 'buts.' Are you trying to question *me*? You've got things topsy-turvy! Hey, Pfeffer!"

The skinny guy turned around. He was busy taking the clock apart. My beautiful clock, with the works showing behind the glass, a clock that goes for three months without winding. It will need a complete repair job now.

"What is it, Boss?" he asked.

The other one sighed. "Pfeffer, am I questioning the gentleman or is the gentleman questioning me? What do you think, Pfeffer?"

Pfeffer raised his eyebrows as though he were thinking it over.

"I wonder . . ." he said.

"Well, this has gone far enough," the boss said. Then to me: "Where are you hiding the stuff? Tell us where it is, and make it snappy!"

"What stuff?" I said.

I swear I didn't have the faintest notion what stuff he was talking about. But he thought I was holding out on him and said so. Then he changed his tack and asked suddenly, "What do you think of Premier Laval's politics?"

What did I think of politics? It seems I should have answered straight off; stopping to think about it proved my ideas were not so good.

"I beg your pardon," I said. "You're the one who says that . . ."

He shrugged his shoulders. "He doesn't even have the courage of his convictions. . . ."

I tried to explain that the question had caught me unawares. No one had ever asked me such a thing before.

"That shows the kind of people you travel with," the fat guy said, very pleased with himself.

The skinny guy grunted to show he thought so too.

It was no use trying to justify myself. I wanted to say that I didn't think anything about Premier Laval's politics, any more than I thought about any other premier's politics. Some people make it their business to worry about politics. Not me. If a man is put at the head of a government, there must be reasons for it. As I don't know what the reasons are, how should I have any ideas about his politics? Whatever his politics are, he was put there to see that they're carried out . . . so . . . Of course, I couldn't explain that to the fat guy. He wouldn't listen. It looked as if he were asking me questions just for the pleasure of hearing his own voice.

By now all Pauline's clothes and mine were lying on the floor. The short guy with the red mustache got on a chair and rummaged in the boxes on the closet shelf. He dragged out some old artificial flowers, a black apron Alfred used to wear when he went to kindergarten, all kinds of odds and ends. The room looked a sight. The two men at the table finished the soup and said, "Well, how about the next course?"

At this they all held their sides. When they finally

stopped laughing, the fat guy pulled his hat down over his eyebrows.

"So it seems you listen to foreign broadcasts?" he said.

There, what did I tell you? An anonymous letter. That's what it was.

"But I don't even listen to the domestic ones," I said, poor innocent that I was.

"Aha! So you don't listen to the domestic broadcasts? Did you hear that, Pfeffer? Our friend here has the gall to boast that he doesn't listen to our domestic broadcasts."

"But . . ."

"No buts. Why is it you don't listen to our domestic broadcasts and you do listen to the foreign ones? Do you find them more interesting? Better informed, perhaps? More entertaining? Some crust!"

"What do you expect me to listen with?" I finally got in.

"With what? Stop the clowning! With what, he asks! With my hindside, maybe . . . with your radio set, you fool!"

"But I have no hindside."

The words just came out like that. I was trying to say I have no radio set. They hit the roof.

"Look here, you old goat, are you trying to be funny? How would you like it if I took you up on it and made sure you had no hindside?"

I got red as a beet and apologized as best I could. But they got me so muddled, I didn't know what I was saying. I meant that I didn't have any radio so I couldn't listen to our domestic broadcasts.

"Sure, if you have no radio. . . . That's to be seen. But if you have no radio, how do you manage to listen to foreign broadcasts?"

"Exactly. I ask you how."

"You ask me! Pfeffer, he asks me! Everything's topsy-turvy again. Who's asking who? Try to keep your place, now. I asked you how you listen to foreign broadcasts."

"But I don't!"

The fat guy let out a long whistle. "Can you beat that? It took you plenty of time to figure that one out. You don't, eh? They all say the same thing. You might use a little imagination."

"But I don't need any imagination."

"You always need it. Especially in the spot you've gotten yourself into."

"But what spot?"

"Will you get it into your head that I'm the one who asks the questions? Come here, Madame."

Pfeffer pushed Pauline beside me. Several of them still stood around, like candlesticks, not saying a word. I wanted to tell her not to worry, that everything would come out all right, that it was an anonymous letter. But Pfeffer clapped his hand over my mouth and snarled, "None of that, you! No coaching!"

At that point the redhead, who had been messing around with the curtains, let one fall down. It was pitiful.

The fat guy started pestering Pauline about domestic broadcasts, foreign broadcasts.

When she swore we had no radio, he yelled, "You say that because you heard your husband say it!"

I tried to explain that it would have been the first time any such thing had happened in thirty-five years but no one paid any attention to me.

"You can see for yourself that we have no radio," Pauline said.

His hat slid backwards on his red neck, uncovering a bald spot. He lifted his right forefinger and shook it at her.

"A little logic, Madame, if you please. How do you expect me to *see* something that's not here? That's a woman for you. Pfeffer, there are two things you must never ask of a woman: logic or the time."

"Especially when you wreck the clock!"

It was true, but Pauline's nerve gave me gooseflesh. I

admired her. I've been admiring her and she's been irritating me for thirty-five years.

"Madame, mind what you say. Wrecked the clock, indeed. It's easy to say . . ."

"And easy to do."

". . . but it would have to be proved. How do I know the clock worked? Why, you may even have hidden leaflets in it."

"How could I hide anything in it when you can see all the works through the glass?"

"Very clever, Madame. Very. We didn't expect such pertinent remarks from you."

Pauline flew off the handle because she thought he had said "impertinent." I had to stop her and tell her she was putting herself in the wrong, although we'd done nothing bad. Then Pauline switched her anger to me. It didn't help a bit.

"Well, how about coming back to those foreign broadcasts?" said the fat guy. "You claim you don't listen to them because you have no radio."

That seemed perfectly clear to me. But it didn't to him.

"You say 'I have no radio' and you think that's all there is to it. But . . ."

He pulled up the armchair and leaned forward with both hands on his thighs. I noticed he was wearing a gold chain on his left wrist. "But . . . can you prove to me you have no radio?"

"You can see for yourself."

"It's not up to me to prove it," he said solemnly. "It's up to you." He pointed his finger at me and then at Pauline.

"A fine thing it would be if I was the one who had to prove that you have no radio! How should I know whether you have one or not? You'll say I don't see one. Is that a reason? First of all, I didn't look. . . ."

He let his eyes wander over the mess in the room.

"My men have only searched the place superficially,"

he added, with a smile. "Anything in the kitchen, Petit-point?"

Petitpoint and the other guy who had got away with the soup were going through the kitchen drawers. They both answered together, "Nothing, Boss," with their mouths full. I can't imagine what they dug up, things being as they are. But Pauline is always hiding away provisions that she somehow manages to scrape up.

"So what does that prove?" the fat guy went on. "Your radio may be somewhere else, being repaired. You were forewarned, so you sneaked it out. Besides, you didn't seem very surprised when we came in. You had your answers all ready."

"I swear we . . ."

"Don't swear. It's not nice. You always regret it later. Come now, admit you listen to foreign broadcasts, that we haven't been wasting our time, or yours."

Suddenly, he was friendly and good-natured.

"Now confidentially, it's no great crime to listen to foreign broadcasts. Everybody does it. We know it very well. And it's very understandable. They're more inter-esting than our own broadcasts, better informed, more entertaining."

But I was stubborn. "I don't know anything about it, since I don't listen to our broadcasts."

He lifted his arms with a shrug: "What's the use of putting on an act *among ourselves*? The war has lasted too long. You get bored. I know how it is. So one day, just by chance, while you're sitting by the radio . . ."

"But I have no radio!"

"Don't keep interrupting me all the time. It's not po-lite. So, as I was saying, one day, just by chance, while you're sitting by the radio, you turn the dial, you run into some static, you try to get rid of it. You can't hear very well and you want to hear better. You don't mean any harm. It's a kind of a game. A man isn't a con-spirator just because he listens to foreign broadcasts. On that basis, you'd have to suppose that the whole country is full of them. That, by the way, is not far from the truth. But, anyway, it's not so very serious. No harm intended. Well, do you confess?"

I shook my head. Then his voice changed, became threatening. "You refuse to admit the facts? Very well. You've not seen the last of us. After the suspicious way you talked about Premier Laval . . ."

"Now, look . . ."

"I won't look. This has gone far enough. That's why the country's in such a state. So many people talk against Premier Laval. That's a *test*. You probably don't even know what a *test* is. Pfeffer, he doesn't know what a *test* is."

He shrugged with a tired, discouraged air. Had I known what a *test* was, I still wouldn't have had a chance to tell him. He was talking for Pfeffer's benefit now. "You see, Pfeffer, when you've been in this game as long as I have you'll sometimes lose patience with the kind of people we run into in the line of duty. Intellectually speaking, tch . . . tch . . . tch . . . They're all mixed up. You constantly have to lower yourself to their level, chose words they can understand. The poverty of their vocabulary, Pfeffer, is beyond belief. How can you expect to get anywhere with them? And the French language is such a model of clarity and simplicity. Just think of the German language! An officer of the Feldgendarmerie was telling me the other day that in German they have words of seventy letters. Can you imagine? And look at these idiots with a plain little French four-letter word."

He stopped, as though struck by a sudden doubt.

"Four letters, Pfeffer. . . . But I expected you to make some comment. A little French four-letter word. How about it?"

Pfeffer looked very worried. What was the boss driving at? A four-letter word? He didn't know whether he was supposed to laugh. He glanced towards the other men, the ninepins. They didn't help him.

"A little *French* word, Pfeffer. How ignorant you are! It's not French, it's English! Come now, don't look so shocked. You can still use English words without being an Anglophile. For instance, the word *trust*. . . . Well, that's an English word. Yet it's a word that belongs in the vocabulary of our National Movement. They must be identified to be fought properly. *Trusts,* not *tests,* of course. You're a nitwit, Pfeffer."

Pauline made the mistake of interrupting him. It's what she always does, I tell her, but she won't listen to me.

"Talking of *trusts,*" she said. "Are you going to beat it?"

I must admit it was very rude and didn't make any sense. The fat guy and Pfeffer started to bluster. I tried to say something. "Pauline's like that, Inspector. For thirty-five years . . ."

"Maybe you've stood for it for thirty-five years," he yelled, "but I won't take it for thirty-five seconds!"

Just then, the two in the kitchen came out with a bottle of oil. Petitpoint was in seventh heaven.

"You see, Boss, black market. There's nearly a quart of oil here."

"It's only a small bottle," Pauline said, "and it's my July ration."

The fat guy wouldn't listen. "Black market," he said, "black market. They listen to foreign broadcasts and they buy oil on the black market!"

At that point, I got into the argument. It was too silly. I didn't put it that way, you understand, because I began to realize it wouldn't do any good. The fat guy was waving his arms around. "I'll confiscate it! Yes, I will! When the whole country is short of fats. . . . That cooks your goose!"

Pauline was heartbroken. Her oil . . .

"This is the limit!" shouted the fat guy. "Plot all you like, but don't starve the poor. France will never recover as long as there are people like you!"

Again his voice changed in that strange way he had. "Come, now, tell me who sold you this oil."

"Surely," said Pauline. "Madame Delavignette."

"Did you hear that, Pfeffer? Delavignette. Dela . . ."

"Yes, Madame Delavignette, our grocer," said Pauline.

"The one on this street?"

"Sure. Next door. Naturally, since she's our grocer."

"And how much did you pay for it?"

"I don't recall now. Let's see . . ."

"Eight hundred francs a quart, huh?"

"Are you crazy? Oh! . . . I'm sorry, Inspector."

That started them off again. They piled a lot of stuff on the writing table: my old notebook, the gas bills, the bottle of oil, a detective story that they thought was suspicious because it was called *The Vichy Murder*, and some odds and ends. One of the silent ones was sweating over a statement for me to sign. I wanted to read it before signing. That's not done either, I found. Finally, I signed to get rid of them. The fat guy took the paper and blew on the signature. Then he held it away from his face to read it. He frowned. He looked at it again. And then he let loose: "What's this tomfoolery? What did you sign there?"

I bent over. "My name," I said. "Unfortunately, that's my name."

"What do you mean, unfortunately? Do you claim your name is . . ."

"Pétain. Robert Pétain. Yes, it's been a nuisance in the neighborhood. But I can't help it. It's my name. Oh, we're not related."

The Inspector was in a stew. Did he give it to me! At last I took my identification papers out, to show him I wasn't fooling, that it really was my name and my father's before me, poor man. If he'd known, he would have changed it. But when my father was young, it was just a name like any other.

"That's enough from you," he said, shoving his hat over his eyes. "Your cracks aren't funny. But if your name is what you say it is, then who is Sellières, Simon Sellières? You claim it's not you? How annoying! Are you sure? We were supposed to search the apartment of a certain Sellières, Simon. Let's see now, what number is this?"

"Number?"

"I mean the house number."

"Eighteen."

"Damn! This Sellières lives at sixteen."

Then Pauline, as usual, thought she could get the upper hand. She started shouting, "So you can't even count up to eighteen and you come around breaking into people's homes . . ."

Again, she didn't make sense, because house numbers don't go consecutively from one to eighteen, but by odd or even numbers. And suppose they could count to eighteen, it still wouldn't give them the right to go breaking into houses. The fat one told her off.

"Besides, you signed the statement," he added, "and the investigation will be continued."

It did no good to protest and to say that if I'd known, I wouldn't have signed. I'd signed and that's all there was to it.

"You're sunk," said Pauline. "It's just like you."

In half a shake, Big Hat had his ninepins assembled. They were gone as fast as they'd come. But with them went the oil, the gas bills, and some cookies they found at the last minute. The skinny guy went out last. Holding the door-knob in his claw, he turned around towards us and said, "Hr-rumph!" That was their last word.

The house was in a fine state. An unholy mess! What made it look so dreadful was the curtain and the pillow feathers. I looked sadly at the empty bottle (no more wine until Tuesday) and the empty soup plates.

Pauline was furious. Everything was my fault. The names she didn't call me! She griped most about the business of Madame Janneau's boyfriend. "Sure," she said, "he was a friend of the Picherelles. But why did you have to get the Picherelles mixed up in it? Why did you have to mention them in front of the police?" I couldn't see why I shouldn't mention them.

"You know very well," she said. "Don't make yourself out a greater fool than you are. Their son is with de Gaulle."

"Well, they couldn't tell that from an old photo. Besides, the man in the snapshot was only a friend of theirs. He got run over or caught pneumonia or something."

Suddenly Pauline lost all interest in the Picherelles. I was about to open a window to let some fresh air in, but she stopped me.

"Leave the window alone," she said and rushed into the kitchen towards the back wall. I looked at the time. Good heavens, of course! Then we sat down next to the gas stove, our ears glued to the wall. From the apartment next door came a booming voice:

"Today, the 753rd day of the str-r-rugle of the French people for their liberation. . . ."

Pauline shook her fist in anger. "The scum!" she said, "They almost made us miss the news!"

Translated by Eugene J. Sheffer

THE MARTYRS, BY THEIR WITNESS

On October 22, 1941, twenty-seven political prisoners were executed near the detention camp at Châteaubriant, in Brittany. They died because a German officer had been killed at Nantes, although not one of them was even accused of having played a part in the assassination. This was the first mass slaughter of hostages in France, and Aragon was one of the first French writers to learn the complete details. He told about their deaths, in a long manuscript written with grief and fury. The manuscript was copied by his associates and smuggled out of the country. At least one of the copies, mailed from Lisbon without signature, reached an American radio station; it was used in many broadcasts to France. Another copy was addressed to Malcolm Cowley, who translated it without knowing that Aragon was the author. A greatly abbreviated version of his translation was printed in Life ("They Die for France," May 25, 1942) and was later included in a volume of eyewitness stories of the war published by Pocket Books. The present version is longer, although it does not include the whole of Aragon's original story.

I SHOULD like nothing better in the world than to have the honor of signing the report that follows. In these days, however, a Frenchman cannot use his name in pleading for the people of his own country. Those who die for France die in secret. It is seldom that the authorities bother to announce their execution, and they never tell why they died. The newspapers are permitted to say only that so many "hostages," so many "terrorists," so many "Communists, Jews, and sympathizers," were guillotined or shot on a certain day. If I can tell how twenty-seven of them died, at Châteaubriant, it is because some of these men asked me to write the story. This letter should be signed with their names, not my own.

In the camp at Châteaubriant, in Brittany, there were in October 1941 a few more than 400 political prisoners, most of them held as Communists or under suspicion of being Communists. All had been prisoners for months and a few had been arrested at the outbreak of the war. Life in the camp had been dragging on as before, except for the well-substantiated rumor that several men would shortly be released. Then, on October 20, a Monday, the prisoners heard that a German officer had been assassinated at Nantes, forty miles away.

About one o'clock in the afternoon, an officer from the German commandant's headquarters conferred with the director of the camp. It was a question of picking out hostages. Some 200 case records were handed over to the sub-prefect's secretary, who would take them to the Ministry of the Interior in Paris. There the hostages would be chosen.

But why call them hostages? Back in the days when there were still rules of warfare, hostages were prominent people named in advance to suffer the consequences of acts committed by their fellow citizens against the enemy. In this case, it was after the act that the so-called hostages were chosen, among prisoners who had nothing to do with killing or plotting to kill a German officer. And they were handed over to the enemy by the Ministry of the Interior of a government that calls itself French —a government that obligingly drew up a list of Frenchmen for the Germans to execute.

That same Monday evening, German sentries were posted outside the camp in place of the Gardes Mobiles. The prisoners were confined to barracks until nine o'clock the following morning. About nine in the evening, the sentries fired on the camp, thinking they saw a shadow.

A bullet whistled past the ears of a prisoner sleeping in Barrack 10. The German guards were relieved on Tuesday morning. All day rumors were running about. People said that thirty hostages were to be named in the camp; also they said—on the strength of an indiscreet remark by a Garde Mobile—that most of the victims would be taken from Barrack 19, where there were only twenty-one men. About nine o'clock Tuesday evening, the German sentries returned.

Afterwards I saw a letter from one of the surviving prisoners in Barrack 19. "We talked pretty late into the night," he said, "and nobody had any illusions about what was going to happen. The principal subject we discussed was, 'Will we be guillotined or shot?' During the night another sentry fired at an imaginary shadow. Most of us managed to get to sleep towards morning. . . .

"On Wednesday morning at nine o'clock," the letter continues, "we went to get our coffee. Everyone could feel and almost see the threat that hung over the camp. About ten the sub-prefect, Lieutenant Moreau, and Second Lieutenant Touya passed our barrack and went to look at the gate of the camp that opens on the main highway. They seemed to be discussing whether it was big enough for trucks to use. A few minutes later Second Lieutenant Touya assembled his gendarmes to give them new orders. All were posted in the camp, and the squad that had been dismissed was brought back by an order that reached the men on their way to barracks. Most of us visited Camp P-1; it was the last chance that many of us would have to see our friends. At noon we set the table and Ploumarch cooked a fish that his family had sent him. Michels helped him, with no less dignity than he showed in the Chamber of Deputies."

A second letter gives other details of the lunch in Barrack 19. Timbault had decided to contribute all his provisions to one good meal. "And what about your three packs of tobacco," somebody asked him. "Hadn't we better smoke them too?" Ploumarch got himself scolded

~ 138 ~

for having forgotten to heat the tea water. "Quit dreaming and put it on the fire, or we won't have time for our tea." It was too late then, and the water never came to a boil.

Going back to the first letter, we read: "Barthélemy, who shared my table, was writing a letter to his family. Stopping to look out the window, he gave a cry of surprise. Through the picket fence that separated us from Camp P-2, we could see a squad of gendarmes standing at attention and facing the gate. Second Lieutenant Touya opened the gate. Followed by a German officer and the gendarmes, he marched straight to our barrack. He opened the door, stood for a moment saluting us, then walked in with the German.

" 'Greetings, gentlemen,' he said with a show of great politeness. 'Please be ready to step out when your name is called.' "

"We were ready, all of us standing in front of my bed, which was the first to the left as one entered. The second lieutenant began reading from a list: Michels, Timbault, Ploumarch, Barthélemy . . . fifteen names in all. The sixteenth was Delavaquerie, and this time nobody stepped forward. 'He's in Camp P-1,' somebody said after a short silence. The lieutenant turned and walked out, closing the door behind him. There were six of us left, and we looked at each other like men returned from the dead. . . ."

In Barrack 10, we learn from another letter, the lieutenant "stood for a moment in the doorway, looked around with a sickly smile, then quickly uttered a single name: Guy Moquet. That name was like the blade of a guillotine on all our necks, like a bullet in all our hearts." Moquet, an overgrown, light-hearted boy of seventeen, was the most popular of all the prisoners.

After the other victims had been collected—no more than one or two from each barrack except the first—the gendarmes marched into the infirmary and came out with Gardette, who could scarcely walk. There were now twenty-seven hostages, and they were taken to Barrack 6, in the center of Camp P-2, where each of them was given an envelope and a sheet of paper to write his last message. One hostage named Kérivel asked and was granted permission to say goodbye to his wife, who was a prisoner in the same camp.

Now, in all the barracks, prisoners were waiting. All the windows were crowded with men standing on beds and tables pushed against the wall. The parish priest of Béré was seen entering the camp. People whispered that the priest of Châteaubriant would have nothing to do with the Germans. Mme. Kérivel passed by, on her way to see her husband. Hope had vanished. At 2:25 the priest emerged from Barrack 6; at 2:30 the German trucks appeared on the highway. Then from Barrack 6 a song rose: the Marseillaise. The whole camp joined in.

At three oclock, the three German trucks were standing in front of Barrack 6. The lieutenant opened the door and called the roll once more. As each name was called, a man stepped forward. The gendarmes emptied all his pockets, tied his hands together, and made him climb into one of the trucks. Each truck took nine hostages. They raised their bound hands to the other prisoners, whom they saw at the windows, and all the time they kept on singing the Marseillaise. *"Ils viennent jusque dans nos bras égorger nos fils et nos compagnes."*

Dr. Ténine called from his truck to the German officer, "It is an honor for us French to be killed by German bullets." Then he pointed to Moquet and said, "But it is a crime to shoot a boy of seventeen."

I have seen many of the prisoners' letters telling what happened that afternoon, and I wish I could quote them all, for each adds new details. One man tells how those in his barrack thought they could recognize Timbault's loud voice and Moquet's young voice among the singers. "Through the cracks in the wooden fence," the letter continues, "we could see shadows moving. We guessed that our comrades were climbing into the trucks and we crowded to the north windows to see them go. The gendarmes were still there, posted every ten yards. Farther away, under the watch towers at the gate, we could see the dark figures of German soldiers with helmets and rifles. A cart drove in the gate; it was the milkmaid. A gendarme took her horse by the bridle, turned it around, and slapped it on the rump. The air was mild and the sky exceptionally clear for late October. Nobody stirred outside the barracks, orders being faithfully observed, but Kiki, our fox terrier, rolled in the grass, enjoying the sun. At last the motors started; the trucks were going to leave. We heard the Marseillaise once more from the other side of the fence, and this time the rest of us joined in, barrack by barrack, until the whole camp was singing. . . . The gendarmes stood at attention and presented arms as the trucks moved out of the camp. Our comrades were dying with military honors."

At this moment all the prisoners came out of the barracks. Four hundred of them were standing on the parade ground and singing—two verses and two choruses of the Marseillaise. Second Lieutenant Touya, who a moment before had shaken the hand of the German officer who led away the twenty-seven hostages, looked worried and embarrassed, but he kept pointing to the German sentry and at last he blew his whistle. The prisoners, who had been whispering instructions to each other, suddenly stopped singing, and the silence that fell on the executioners was more impressive than the songs. The lieutenant could not refuse to give a few items of information, which passed from group to group together with the list of hostages. Touya had said that the hostages would be shot at 4:15. Immediately the prisoners decided to reassemble at that moment.

At 4:15 they were all standing outside the barracks as if for a rollcall, their heads uncovered, in silence. The names of the hostages were called, and at each name a comrade answered, "Shot."

Of the evening that followed, there is nothing to report except the courage of Mme. Kérivel. When she had come to the barrack of the condemned men to say good-bye to her husband, she was seized with pity at the sight of Guy Moquet. She proposed to the officers that she should take his place. She wished to die with her husband and let the boy live. Her offer had been refused. Now in the darkness she walked up and down the open space between the women's barracks with other women prisoners. She said to them, "Why should we beat our breasts? We didn't come here to pick flowers. Life goes on." A little later she said, "Above all, go ahead with the entertainment we are planning for Sunday. Nothing must be changed." All evening she talked in this fashion, and it was only in the barrack that she began sobbing. The following morning she was as erect and brave as ever.

On Thursday the prisoners learned the details of the execution. It took place in a sand pit two kilometers north of Châteaubriant. The hostages had been driven through town singing the Marseillaise. The townspeople took off their hats as they passed. At the farm near the sand pit, the peasants were placed under house arrest by the Germans, the doors and shutters were closed, and a machine gun was aimed at the door.

In the sand pit there were three rows of nine stakes each. The executions were carried out in three volleys, at 3:55, at 4:00, and at 4:10. The twenty-seven victims insisted on going to their death with their hands untied and without bandages on their eyes. They sang till the last moment, and shouted, *"Vive la France!* Hurrah for Soviet Russia! Hurrah for the Communist Party!" Dr. Ténine told the officer commanding the firing squad, "You are going to see how a French officer dies." And big Timbault, the metal worker, stood facing the ten Germans who were aiming at him and cried, "Hurrah for the German Communist Party!" As he climbed down from the truck, he had asked a gendarme to give him a light "to smoke my last cigarette"; then he said something to Second Lieutenant Touya that nobody over-heard but the other men who were about to die. The gendarmes reported that Touya turned pale.

The gendarmes also brought back keepsakes which they turned over to the prisoners: one man's watch, an-other man's ring, a letter from a third. They shared the feeling of horror that reigned in the camp and the town. The mayor of Châteaubriant refused to let the bodies be buried in the packing boxes that the Germans had fur-nished instead of coffins. That night the bodies stayed in the town hall. Coffins were provided in the morning. One detail that the gendarmes reported: one of the bodies was too big for its coffin. A German took a crow-bar to force it in. When the town gravedigger pro-tested, the German growled, "*Kommunist, pas Français. Heraus.*" That day the coffins were distributed to various cemeteries in the neighborhood, three by three. Families can visit the graves, but they do not know which is theirs, for the coffins had no name on them.

On the day after the execution, the people of the neighborhood began making pilgrimages to the sand pit. The stakes were still standing, and there were dark stains in the sand. On Sunday, October 26, the stakes had been removed, but more than five thousand people walked through the sand pit and dropped flowers.

All these stories were brought to camp by the gen-darmes, who also told other details of the execution. It seems that Guy Moquet, who had yielded to tears before leaving camp, but whose courage on the road had been as great as that of the others, had fainted on entering the sand pit. Tied to the stake, he had been shot without regaining consciousness. I saw a copy of his last letter, addressed to his mother: "Certainly I don't want to die, but what I wish with all my heart is that my death may serve some purpose. . . . A last goodbye to all my friends, and to my little brother—tell him to study and learn to be a man. Seventeen and a half years, my life has been short, I have no regrets."

On all Saints' Day, November 1, the pilgrimages recommenced: a great wreath of flowers was placed where each stake had stood in the sand pit, and other wreaths were carried to the new graves in the cemeteries. The German authorities forebade these pilgrimages and tried to discover the identity of the "culprits" who had brought the flowers. They discovered nothing.

Translated by Malcolm Cowley

INTRODUCTION TO 33 SONNETS
COMPOSED IN SOLITARY CONFINEMENT

By Jean Noir

Presented by François la Colère

The author of the 33 Sonnets here presented by Aragon is Jean Cassou, who chose the appropriate pseudonym of Jean Noir for his underground writings. While in solitary confinement in one of the most dreadful prisons in France, Cassou composed these poems in his head, and was only able to write them down on his release. Circulated at first through underground channels, they were at length brought out in Paris by the Editions de Minuit, a clandestine publishing house which conducted a large and flourishing business under the very noses of the Vichy French and the occupation authorities.

I

In those days France was a drifting raft loaded with castaways; provisions were short, the children were pale, the women rent the air with their cries, and the men were so thin that their stiff joints were clearly visible as they stared balefully, dry-eyed, at the horizons without sails. In short, you may at your leisure complete the whole allegory of the new Medusa * yourselves, since the world in which you live is still like a barren sea, and

* The reference is to *The Raft of the Medusa*, the famous painting by Géricault in the Louvre.

creatures of flesh and blood about you are still being martyrized by the thousands. O poets, you can make of this world whatever your frenzied imagination bids you (each in his turn); without stooping to invention, you will find all around you the monsters that are supposed to issue only from your tormented brains, you may . . .

But that was not what I wanted to say.

When on some fabulous plague-ridden ship, its dread flag flying at the mast, wallowing in the troughs of an uncharted sea, the last hale passengers appear on the promenade deck or in the first-class saloon, pretending to be still in the land of the living, or gather together to play a ghostly, ceremonial game of whist—when, on some such doomed schooner, or steamer lost in the ice floes, some ocean liner without bearings, the travelers hear the agonized groans of their companions rising from the cabins and the hold, when they have, in short, exhausted all the emotional possibilities of the no-trumps of misery or of a pointless discard, with what delight do they welcome the slightest and most ambiguous jest, the least pun of a steward, the idiotic "I see you" of some specter playing hide-and-seek in the passageways, or the practical jokes in the dining room. . . . It was in this spirit that the public threw itself upon a book by M. Anatole de Monzie, who should bear the Christian name of "Punch," if he works on behalf of darker powers which are well known to us.

Now in this book, *The Season of Judges*, which appeared in the summer of 1943, at a moment when everyone was exasperated by long waiting, when our young people, thrown to the Minotaur, resolved to accept their fate grimly, when trains were being blown up, killing became a ritual, and the gentle land of France was being transformed into an inferno, in *The Season of Judges* M. de Monzie devotes only a short chapter, somewhat less than thirteen pages, to "Our Prisons." Of these, six pages are allotted to a personal experience, rather mild, of the German barracks at the line of demarcation, one and a half to the *model* prison of Monaco, where he says Verlaine and Oscar Wilde were confined for a period (!), and the rest to Fort-Barraux, of which *Toute la Vie* of April 28, 1942, said, according to M. de Monzie, "It is like life in a château with movies every week." Moreover the author seems to speak of *our* prisons only as a psychologist, remarking that it is bad for our delinquents to be condemned to idleness, and that idleness is the worst, the most demoralizing aspect of *our* penal system. And that is all that this would-be Chief Justice (when Vichy falls) found to deplore in the penal *system* of *our* government, which, as he says, provides only "*a lazy solution for obligatory laziness, an example of paternalism.*"

What a strange, what a very strange jest, O ship-wrecked men, my brothers. . . . People fought for copies of *The Season of Judges* at station bookstalls, everywhere it was devoured with the hunger of meatless days, with teeth sharpened by chewing air. Some found it not too bad, rather interesting in fact; it was discussed by people in the queues. . . . Nobody lingered much, however, over the chapter on the prisons, which seemed so much rose-water after the book by Silvio Pellico and other classics in the field. He nonetheless reassured many of those whose sleep from time to time was uneasy at the thought of half a million Frenchmen in chains.

For on the boat I was describing, where the rules of good society are still seemingly observed, on the raft of the new Medusa, it is not the hallucinations of Géricault that haunt the readers of M. de Monzie. And yet . . .

And yet when cotton-wool is no longer to be found at the druggist's, with what wax do these Adhémars, these Cunégondes stuff up their ears? Carried away by the storm, they seem to know nothing of the prisons among which they pass, save what this elegant Anatole, this reformer who devotes himself to trimming the brush along the road, is willing to tell them, and this at a time when five hundred thousand Frenchmen are in danger of acquiring bad habits. . . .

And yet the walls are not so thick, the gags are not so tight, the general fear is not so crass, that one may not hear from time to time the sighs, the cries of revolt, the songs and the sobbings. To you and me, to anyone who listens, the wind that blows over this land is laden with the clanking of irons, with voices crying out from behind bars, a clamor that nothing can subdue, a terrible ear-piercing lament that defies bolts and jailers. Listen.

II

However guarded the secret, however perfectly silence may be maintained, there are names that bring a shiver even to Frenchmen who at first glance seem most impassive, most absorbed in their business, with a crease in their trousers and a decoration in their buttonholes. Just whisper in their ears the words Gurs, Drancy, Fresnes, or Montluc, and you will note by the expression on their respectable faces that these names mean something to them, although such things are never mentioned either in the newspapers or on the Marshal's radio broadcasts.

Indiscretions have evidently been committed, for even I can tell you something about Gurs, from which a friend of mine has been released after having been sent up presumably for a fifty-year term. I shall long remember his voice in the hotel room that wintry day as he described life in the hovels of this cursed camp, on a windy plateau where the slightest depression in the earth oozed water. The men went about in tatters, with at best an old tin can to drink from, and when there was a sort of typhus epidemic the medic required that the patients carry their own stools away. But what was there to put them in? Only the tin can from which they were obliged to drink afterwards. Then too there were the mobile guards, drunk from noon on, who made a sport of charging with fixed bayonets at the wretches who let down their breeches between the huts because there were no privies. . . . Gurs, a strange syllable, like a sob that comes from no throat. . . .

And Drancy. They tell all sorts of stories about Drancy, of hunger, humiliation, and beatings there. When I think of Drancy with its tall buildings, its cheap skyscrapers where the water freezes in the conduits, set in the midst of a vast desolate plain dotted with cabins and dreary gardens, I find it hard to imagine what the mere word Drancy must mean to thousands of men and women today. Perhaps I have heard exaggerated tales. And yet I know of a woman of eighty-three, the mother of a friend of mine, who was beaten *because she trembled while putting on her stockings* when they came to haul her off to Drancy in the middle of the night. Things did not move fast enough to suit her captors.

Everyone has some intimate experience of the monstrous torture that goes on: a cousin who was sent all across France with manacled hands, a sister in the Santé Prison, a schoolmate whose legs were broken at the Hotel Terminus in Lyons, a relative who happened to be at Mont-Valérien when some of the prisoners sang the Marseillaise all one morning, until the bullets came to interrupt their song forever. (Their only regret was that they had forgotten some of the verses.) Each of us has some personal testimony, not to mention the news from Germany, Poland, from those regions of horror, those concentration camps in which people are thrown for refusing to turn traitor, or for less, for the kind of nose they had or might have had. Not to mention the third degree, the pincers, the burned feet, the boot torture, the whippings, the needles driven into testicles, the men flayed alive. Not to mention other things which seem so exaggerated that those who have escaped exhibit their scars in silence and the executioners themselves send home the bodies of their victims in sealed coffins.

A prison among thousands is the jail at Saint-Etienne.

It was there that Henry Lagrange of Limoges, twenty-five years old, Molet de Béziers, twenty-two, and Delorme, secretary of the miners' union of Saint-Etienne, forty-six, died of starvation at the beginning of 1943. Their daily food ration consisted of a piece of bread, two bowls of rutabaga or Jerusalem artichokes, and six spoonfuls of water, called soup. All the other prisoners, whether thieves or murderers, had the right to receive four packages of food a month, of three kilograms each, which permitted them to survive. But Lagrange, Molet, Delorme, and their like, being Communists, came under the ministerial decree of October 26, 1942, and were entitled to receive only one package of four kilos a month. Eight kilos less to eat for the crime of believing in Communism instead of killing one's father or raping little girls. . . .

At the Saint-Etienne prison, three men occupied each tiny cell, four meters long and three wide, with only two beds among them. Every day for three-quarters of an hour the prisoners were permitted to walk in the yard, a triangular enclosure six meters long on each side, with walls so high the sun never reached the bottom. The slop-pails in the cells were hardly ever cleaned or disinfected. The mess-tins were sent from one cell to another, for all to eat from, without being washed. A few cases of typhoid fever brought about no serious attempt at sanitation. One shower bath a week was the rule. The prisoners became such skeletons that the new arrivals shuddered, knowing the fate in store for themselves. . . .

At the Saint-Etienne prison the traffic in ration books went on merrily. When the scandal became public, all the bookkeepers and three of the guards were removed. . . . The story was hushed up, but Lagrange, Molet, and Delorme had died of starvation. They had less right to eat than parricides, forgers, or spies.

It is only one of many prisons. I have singled it out solely because irrefutable evidence about it has come into my hands. It is only an average prison, average in its horrors and injustices, neither better nor worse than the others. . . .

M. de Monzie did not go there.

III

Undoubtedly some readers will object to my having used this particular example in speaking of our penal system: the case of a few Communists. I shall be accused of making distinctions between the Patriots, but what can I do? It was not I who introduced such distinctions in the ministerial decree of October 26, 1942, but M. Barthélemy, nor was it I who denied the Communists the right to a lawyer to represent them, but M. Gabolde. It is M. Barthélemy, it is M. Gabolde who sought to divide the ranks of the Patriots, and I am compelled to protest first against the greater injustice. Nor do I distinguish between the kinds of blood that have been shed in fighting the enemy: Gaullist or Communist, Jewish or Christian, it is always just as red. Nor do I intend, in this long preamble, to lead up to the case of a Communist, as will presently be seen. I flatter myself that a day will come, and quite soon too, when these quarrels will seem strange, like those of the monks of the year 1000.

Let me explain this analogy. In a work by M. Emile Mireaux, who was the second-rate collaborator of Pétain in what the Marshal euphemistically calls his Finances, but who is also a historian, one may read how that monument of our poetic heritage, the *Chanson de Roland*, was born of the quarrels between the monks of Cluny and the Cistercian friars. It survived those quarrels, now so puerile to our eyes, since the Cistercians and monks of Cluny both had no other object but to advance the greatness of the Church. Let no one then set the Patriots of today against one another, when they are as one for France. Out of their common struggle, even if no epic has as yet appeared, it is nevertheless true that some admirable outcries have been heard, and works as vibrant as the struggle itself have been produced. It matters little whether these come from the side of Cluny or the Cistercians, so long as they speak above all with the voice of France.

You may believe that I am wandering from the subject with my talk of the *Chanson de Roland,* but that is because you do not know what underlies this allusion. For Joseph Bédier the *chansons de geste,* including that of Roland, came into being in the sanctuaries that mark the route of the great pilgrimages along the roads of France, above all the road to Santiago de Compostella, which belonged to the order of Cluny. Today, however, the epic of France is being forged in other sanctuaries on the road to the national Calvary. Our most ardent adherents, and here again I refer to no special sect or denomination, are imbued body and soul with their contribution to that great poem of France which refutes Voltaire's notion that our people are wanting in the epic spirit. From the prisons which are the sanctuaries of the Fatherland there rises the new song of Roland, a Roland with a thousand and one heads, whose voice will not crack as he blows on his magic horn. For by now the whole world has heard it, shuddering, and the answer will come.

There are places where the spirit breathes. . . . The old theme of Barrès in *The Sacred Hill* is reborn again in our tragic land; it grows upon us in those pure songs, recently published, that have come from the prison camps in Germany, where nearly two million of our men could not abide so long without giving voice to the sustained music which has made France as the Aeolian harp of the world. *There are places where the spirit breathes,* and if *oflags* and *stalags* must be numbered among them, why should not the many prison camps on French soil give forth a mighty and melodious sigh?

There are places where the spirit breathes. . . . M. de Monzie, after his experience at the demarcation line and from his observations at the model prison of Monaco, concluded that emptiness of hand and heart weighs more heavily on the prisoner than confinement itself, although this is not the way he defines the evil. The remedy he proposes is that prisoners be obliged to manufacture slippers. If he had extended his investigations to cover the prisons at Gurs, Saint-Sulpice, Compiègne, and other such places, he might have learned something of value to a would-be Chief Justice. Some of the prisoners, without the knowledge of their jailers, find a solution for their enforced idleness which is as masterly as it is original. Those who are acquainted with the secret life of the prison camps know that everywhere the indomitable spirit of the Patriots has filled the void not with mechanical labor, but with the organized exercise of their highest faculties by the prisoners themselves. Whosoever has seen the operation of those extraordinary *prisoners' universities* which have sprung up in nearly all the camps and prisons in France has brought back a sense of exaltation and confirmed our belief that places where the spirit breathes are increasing more and more rapidly. From a man who was at Gurs I learned that he gave eighty-four pupils there a course in the origin of the French language, as if this question were the most pressing and exciting of all. And so it was.

However, it is not of these informal universities that I wish to speak here, not of these schools where the flame of France still burns. I want to stop to listen to one special song—not of a solitary singer, for there is no real solitude in the captivity of the Patriots. But still a song that preserves the tone of a particular man, a *human person* as he is called nowadays, whose personal note rises above the great collective contumely in which the prisoner is held. I happen to have heard it escape from one of those places where the spirit will breathe hereafter. And in its way this song, like the prisoners' universities, is definite proof that the spirit is not dead here.

IV

The manuscript before me bears the title: 33 *Sonnets Composed in Solitary Confinement,* and its dedication is "To my prison companions." It is in a sense difficult to discuss it, since however well I know the author, I must say nothing about him until the proper time comes. Hence I am deprived of all the usual aids to criticism, including all comparison with earlier work from the same hand. I must be content to call him Jean Noir.

33 Sonnets Composed in Solitary Confinement. I may remark that the sonnet, that strange challenge to thought and song, polished for four centuries by the most skillful singers, seemed to have reached its peak with Mallarmé. Yet now it reappears at a most unexpected moment, when it is supposedly worn out with age and artifice, coming in a strange manner from a strange place and with a new prestige. Here is a sonnet hailing from the murk of a dungeon, not an academic thing born of witless leisure. A sonnet in the grand mysterious line of French speech, a form of communication in which the writer and poet is no chance rhymester, but one who is profoundly aware of the dark cell that France has become, a poet shaped by events to serve as the sensitive echo of that shadowy underworld. The most tremulous prophecies appear in the work of this man who must remain anonymous, emanations of a current passing through the embattled hearts of the people at every stage of the road to Liberty, the current that nourished *Les Misérables,* and the martyrs of June 1848, whom the young Flaubert saw in chains in Paris, and those who refused to accept the armistice of '71 and sang in the face of death, the whole mighty current rising from the depths of an art that is native to France. This is the work of a real artist, I would say, for among our writers there are few who are artists in his sense. In all that Jean Noir writes there resounds a diapason of the people, even when he seems most to depart from common ways, as if his artful song were infused with the melodies of two-penny street ballads. This strange duality mirrors another duality: there is the man I used to meet in the streets, with whom I shook hands, who had his name in the telephone directory, and there is the entirely different character revealed in these poems, who will always be an ardent youth, no matter how gray his hair, a man of passion for women and for his country. How can I explain him, my Jean Noir, except by comparing him to musicians such as Chopin or Mozart? And yet he is not quite the same, with his hidden fire, his readiness to face tragic events. . . . Yes, what has happened shows us that in his daily life he disguised his real nature, as revealed in his books, which was to make him refuse to accept the armistice of June 1940 from the very beginning, to make him become a soldier of the Liberation, like the heroes he himself created. . . . But I almost forgot that I was to speak only of his sonnets.

It was not by accident that this prisoner chose the sonnet form. . . . He had, alas, nothing to write with, nothing but his memory and time. For ink he had only the night, for writing paper only his retentive mind. He had to memorize each poem . . . until the uncertain day when he would leave the prison. He needed not only to write each poem, but to learn it. The fourteen lines of the sonnet, the perfection of their sequence, the suitability of their rhymes for memorization, all that devolved upon the poet not as a matter of verbal acrobatics but as the inevitable frame imposed by the historic circumstances under which his thought came to him. Henceforth it will be almost impossible not to see in every sonnet the expression of liberty under constraint, of thought imprisoned. 33 *Sonnets Composed in Solitary Confinement* stand at the misty borderland of poetry, an unrivaled document of man and his dreams in chains, of that which never can be chained.

I shall speak of the poignant and inaccessible quality of these sonnets, though they are direct and unfeigned. I shall speak to those who through over-anxiety to learn something about the writer may close the book without discerning therein our own muffled voice, the buried flame of our hidden life.

I shall speak of these sonnets not only as born in irons, but as the negation of those irons, and not only because the poet was a son of France but because he sang the song of France. I beg you to hear him.

V

Oh! ce soir soit pour nous le dernier soir tombé,
Et puisqu'il faut rêver, rêvons la mort des rêves.

From the survivor of a shipwreck those who have never experienced a similar horror expect a description of the terror of the storm, the waves crashing upon the deck, and the agonizing choice between those whom the lifeboats bear to safety and others who are to be left behind. Or at least, as in John Milton, we readily accept his transference of the night of the blind to some *Paradise Lost*. But the poet, by the unexpected grandeur of his obscure designs, sometimes disappoints those who count upon patent symbols or concrete reporting.

If you expect this particular poet to give you prison poetry, a description of the life led there, or the lament that rises from behind these stone walls, these sonnets will mean nothing to you. You will be like a child who does not know how to listen to the murmur of the sea in the shell he holds. Nor can you hope to find here any tribute to the values for which this man was deprived of his freedom. . . .

Since dream we must, ah, dream the death of dreams.

In his sunless prison the captive takes no pleasure in recording his hunger, thirst, cold, pain, or man's cruelty to man. For him a poem is a tool to express defiance of the things he scorns. The poem is for him a superhuman effort to remain human still, to reach to those zones of the spirit and the heart which all who surround him deny and slander. The poem—the sonnet—is not a means of flight, an "escape" as we say nowadays, but a retort, the retort of a man of natural greatness caught in the hands of pygmies, Gulliver throwing off the nets of the Lilliputians. Its beauty, its power, the emotion it conveys derive precisely from the tremendous detachment of this individual with a number, however foul his slop-pail, however he may be insulted and ordered about by brutes —the tremendous detachment of this man abandoning himself to the purity of his interior heaven, of which, these sonnets attest, no one can rob him. (Now it can be understood why earlier I mentioned my friend at Gurs, who taught his fellow prisoners the origins of the French language. Neither he nor Jean Noir, who composed sonnets in his head, was exceptional; both brought a human solution to a superhuman problem, both served as examples of human dignity in the midst of misfortune. Their detachment from their surroundings and the activity chosen by both men are similar. And the example of my friend from Gurs helps me to deny the imputation of escapism in the works of Jean Noir.)

Et puisqu'il faut rêver, rêvons la mort des rêves.

There are several observations to be made upon the relative obscurity of these sonnets: they are obscure in the manner of a soliloquy, with no thought of an auditor, of any other witness than the poet himself, obscure as dreams might be, or rather like the obsessions of insomnia, obscure like a clouded diamond which underneath has all the sparkle of other brilliants, obscure at first, like a vague pain that declares itself in the end. . . . When night has fallen in the cell, what chimeras, what monsters or splendid visions take possession of a prisoner? Reveries, memories, mingling with surmises as to his fate, the future and the past confronted and balanced. Sometimes the most surprising images glisten among the shadows:

> Il n'y avait que des troncs déchirés
> que couronnaient des vols de corbeaux ivres,
> Et le château était couvert de givre
> ce soir de fer où je m'y présentai. . . .

or the lure of still another vision:

> Lorsque nous entrerons cette ville chinoise,
> Je boîterai un peu, mais je connaîtrai l'amour.

It would be absurd to see in these sonnets only the inspiration of those nights of captivity; they are also a projection of the science of language, the poetic meditations of a skilled technician of versification, a modern master of ancient metrical styles brought up to date. One notes also his originality in rhyming, bordering often upon assonance, and his way of introducing words used in common speech (expletives which to an inexperienced eye seem superfluous, but which make for the perfection of the line and the accent, like *donc*). And then, surpassing all else, there is a translation of a poem by Hoffmannsthal.

A sonnet by Hoffmannsthal. A German sonnet given form in French by an imprisoned Patriot. Let no one say that the meeting of the two nations here is in bad taste; that is what makes the episode memorable. The poet has provided a footnote to his translation, from which I quote:

"All reading was forbidden to the prisoners, but one day a page of the *Pariser Zeitung* fell into my hands. My cell-mate and I devoured this infamous sheet; it was at least something to read. I had the pleasure of discovering a sonnet of Hoffmannsthal's there, *Die Beide*, an anthology piece that had always charmed me, and which I managed to adapt into our language in the course of one of my sleepless nights."

It was a spiritual adventure to be long remembered, occurring in the midst of the most terrible of wars, this encounter between Jean Noir and Hoffmannsthal in prison, the two poets fraternizing and by their mutual understanding condemning their jailers and the Germany to whom those jailers gave obedience. It is an adventure to be long remembered, big with the future, and epitomizing the spiritual affinity, the high-mindedness of our heroes and our poets. I can imagine with what pride Jean Noir, imprisoned for having fought the Germans, did his magnificent translation of Hoffmannsthal that night. I can imagine how he felt, and this tells far more than could a faithful description about the indomitable spirit of our French prisoners. Beneath the modesty and reserve maintained by all those who have come closest to the fearful horror of these inexpiable years, before whose martyrs the world will one day stand mute, I perceive the whole heroic harvest that gives France infinitely more than the grandeur that was Rome. . . .

As a background to the soliloquy of these sonnets one must always remember the prison. Each sonnet must be read with the thought, the pain, the fire of a man imprisoned in mind. As I hold this shell to my ear I can hear the endless murmur of the sea, singing of liberty lost through love of liberty:

> *Bruits lointains de la vie, divinités secrètes,*
> *Rumeurs cachées aux plis des épaisseurs muettes.* . . .

For the real world vibrates here too, the real world so close to the drama of these confining walls, the world of which the prisoner catches a glimpse even from the depths of his darkness. . . . No, the prisoner has not shut his eyes to reality, but to his temporary defeat. He has shut his eyes only to see more clearly what was important, to recognize imprisonment as an accident, the prison itself as an accessory, a terrible accessory, but only an accessory to the real world. It is as if he were making a confession when he tells us:

> Les poètes un jour reviendront sur la terre,
> Leurs plus beaux vers enfin délivrés du sanglot
> Qui les fit naître. . . .

For if the prisoner dreams of "the death of dreams," liberty for him means that his best verses may "be freed of the sobs that gave them birth."

May the prison crumble and only the song survive! This song, though written in secret, will long survive all our prisons, and remain, as after the retreat of a great flood, a high-water mark in the great drama of French history.

In the thirty-second sonnet we find the poet's real conclusion: "When scorn has broken every dike, dear heart, near to breaking, all that is left to you is to scorn scorn itself."

And that, perhaps, in a few simple words, is the lesson that France has to give to the world, France in the midst of her misfortunes.

Translated by Hannah and Matthew Josephson

AN APPEAL TO FRENCH INTELLECTUALS

This appeal, printed as a handbill, was one of many such issued by the underground press. Aside from its hortatory tone, which indicates the commanding position taken by French writers during the occupation, it shows the foresight, the preparedness of the underground organization for any emergencies. The National Committee of Writers, led by Aragon in the south, moved swiftly to fill any vacuum left by internal crises or the changing fortunes of war.

THE war has been resumed on the soil of France: on the one hand, the Forces of the Interior are mercilessly harrying the enemy, who is now in the clutches of the Allied armies in Normandy. Never before has the duty of Frenchmen been so clear, and no one will refuse to play his part.

At this significant hour the intellectuals would not want to be left out of the picture. For four years it has been our pride that art, thought, science, and literature have remained free here despite the occupation, a fact that has amazed the whole world. During these decisive weeks, is it possible that we should hear nothing from French intellectuals, whose eternal mission it has been to proclaim what all men long to hear whenever the future is obscure?

The National Committee of Writers greets all the intellectuals of France and urges them to join the valiant company of distinguished men grouped in the National Committees of Doctors, Jurists, Professors, Teachers, and Journalists, groups which have contributed so powerfully to the preservation of our cultural life. The National Committee of Writers today appeals to all these to face the enemy, to parry the measures he has taken to execute his murderous plans.

While Vichy's phantom power was evaporating, and France by every act acknowledged the Provisional Government of the Republic, the invader seized executive power in several French departments. Other departments are now in a state of siege; our country is overrun by savage bands of men who deface, pillage, and kill at pleasure, under the protection of the swastika. The silence of the newspapers and the radio keeps our people in ignorance of what is going on. The brave deeds, as well as the indescribable sufferings of our noblest sons, are hidden from us. This silence is part of Hitler's monstrous plan to destroy France and the French people. This silence is indispensable for the execution of his plan.

To break this silence by all possible means is one of our most essential tasks at this moment.

In a country carved up like ours, each isolated part becomes a kind of fortress. Therefore you, intellectuals, must everywhere take the initiative and speak out, without waiting for orders to come from your various organizations, orders sometimes transmitted slowly or intercepted.

The Writers' Committee appeals to all those who are subject to intellectual discipline from this day forth to create, to stimulate the means of expression for which France thirsts as for fresh water, so that through their efforts newspapers, tracts, bulletins, and pamphlets may spring up everywhere, so that the French spirit may circulate more powerfully through the veins of the people, through the whole agitated body of our country.

To present the news, to tell the truth, to combat the German propaganda mouthed by Vichy, these are things we all can do, and not only the professional journalists among us. All those who live by thought and its expression can serve the cause of liberation in no better way than this. Scholars or artists, laboratory workers or technicians, doctors or lawyers, teachers or philosophers, all of you who use method in your thinking: mobilize your method for the safety of France.

Remember that in our country, divided as it is now, it means a great deal to those who are deprived of their radios, or to the maquis, who have no electricity in their camps, merely to learn the latest news of the Russian offensive, or of the war in Italy, or the directives of the Allied high command. Remember that even the radio cannot know or tell what goes on in your own region except after long delay, and that all around you an epic chapter of French history is being written, a story we cannot afford not to know. Writers, remember that you can find words to galvanize men into action, to give courage in a time of misfortune. Doctors, professors, jurists, engineers, remember that you can put your irreplaceable experience at the disposal of the soldiers in the field and all those who support them. Remember, you who guard the eternal flame of the French spirit, that it is fed by that enormous people's army which is growing every day, by an aroused nation.

The National Committee of Writers asks you to bear in mind that there is no spot in France where the things of the spirit do not flourish. Prove this for yourselves. There are printing presses which will no longer refuse to print what you have to say, while others can be set up somewhere or other, there are hand presses, multigraphing machines; you yourselves have typewriters; statements of value can even be recopied by hand a hundred times. No means of reaching the heart of Frenchmen, of bringing comfort, can or ought to be neglected.

To speak what the enemy would like to conceal is an act of war. To create the organ by which this can be accomplished is to bring arms to our country. The National Committee of Writers urges all those who represent the conscience of France to make the voice of that conscience heard, the song of our land, the cry of our will. Let them take part in the assault on the foreign redoubt established on our soil; let them strike the monster at his most vulnerable point! An argument brought to bear on the hesitant or the bewildered, enlightening those who can no longer see the road ahead, can be a mortal blow to the enemy machine. The timely arrival of news may whip up flagging energy. Whenever a Nazi lie is punctured, human lives are saved.

Let us all get to work then! The hour has struck to bring light to the world, the dawn of a new day, resplendent with the colors of France. The hour has struck when the voice of France will resound throughout the world above the chorus of traitors and the roar of cannon fire.

THE NATIONAL COMMITTEE OF WRITERS
(SOUTHERN ZONE)

Translated by Hannah Josephson

FREE!

(From La Drôme en Armes, August 26, 1944)

Edited by Aragon and his wife, La Drôme en Armes was a clandestine newspaper serving the department of the Drôme. It consisted of four pages, tabloid size, and contained general news of the war, local stories of German atrocities and F.F.I. activity, as well as editorials. Aragon frequently wrote the leader, which was centered on page one. The following is taken from the first number published after the liberation of that area.

FREE! We are going to be free! We hardly dare believe it after all these years of bad news, when the sun rose every day under the sign of death, of heroism which at the time seemed hopeless, of betrayal. Will the horror really end? Are we at last to be delivered from evil?

At any rate we need no longer listen to the pessimists, to the skeptics, to the overcautious. The voices of hope, youth, daring, the demands of the present and the future must be heard again. At last the firing will stop, and the sun will rise and set in an era of peace; men will think no more of destruction, but of rebuilding, of binding up wounds, of living and creating.

To begin with, let us sweep the country clean of the last vestiges of the terrible disease that ravaged us these long years. This is not a matter of revenge, but of hygiene; it is absolutely necessary if we are to begin life over again. Everything contaminated by the Boches must be either disinfected or destroyed, if we would avoid a relapse. A relapse would be too costly.

Among the Frenchmen who were our enemies during these many years there were some weak-spirited people who found the Boches "correct," and could not resist their well-polished boots; there were those who are always drawn to the winner, either out of self-interest, fear, or because force has an irresistible attraction for them; there were others who preferred to be plundered, expropriated, killed, who chose to lose everything they held most dear, sink to the lowest depths of misery and disaster, put their country to fire and sword rather than expose themselves to the "Communist peril"; and there were quite simply the crooks, the criminals, the traitors to all humanity.

And while the men and women of the Resistance, civilians and soldiers, worked tirelessly to undermine the German war machine, these anti-French criticized the Resistance, blocked the Resistance, sold out and betrayed the Resistance. The prisons and concentration camps were full to overflowing, while the Boches and their anti-French collaborators killed, tortured, and deported our people, but the traitors and fools reserved their blame and their curses not for the real criminals, but for the Resistance.

There will be tribunals to rid us of the corrupt, to suppress those who will not yield, and to prevent the infected ones from spreading contagion. But there will remain still some of whom it will be impossible to say whether they are more stupid than evil or more evil than stupid. We must continue to be on guard against slander, against the critics and the doubters. There will still be Frenchmen who will rejoice every time there is a hitch, or because evrything does not run smoothly right away. As if liberation meant a chicken in every pot! As if all men were to become just, kind, and good overnight!

No, throughout the world, and in our ruined and mourning country, there will still be a stupendous job to be done. The first tasks of housecleaning will fall to the Committees of Liberation.

These Committees of National Liberation are to be made up of delegates from all the parties of resistance which were represented in the National Council of Resistance (sitting in Paris and representing the highest civil authority of the country): the National Front, the United Movements of Resistance, the Communist Party, the C.G.T. Outstanding members of the local resistance movements are also to belong to these committees, and if there is room, the representatives of smaller groups or parties which were active against the Boches in their region. The Committees of Liberation will take the place of the municipal council and the mayor. The Departmental Council of Liberation will function as a General Council for the Prefecture.

The task of these Committees of Liberation will be very hard. Therefore, help them and be patient. Consider the endless difficulties that will confront them, the lack of transportation, for example. Think of what the Boches have stolen from us and of all they have destroyed! Remember that our prisoners have not yet returned, remember their fatigue, and our own weariness. . . . Remember the Fifth Column, which will not be exterminated in the twinkling of an eye. Remember all these things, and help your Committees of Liberation to the best of your ability and with all good will!

Civilians of all parties, A.S. and F.T.P., all our glorious French Forces of the Interior, forget your quarrels! Unite so that you may bear cheerfully the heavy tasks ahead of you, so that France may live free and happy!

Translated by Hannah Josephson